"*When Depression Hurts Your Relationship* is an outstanding book, packed with easy-to-read information and strategies that will help couples navigate the stormy waters of depression. Shannon Kolakowski comprehensively tackles how depression negatively roots itself in the bonds of a partnership and offers solutions that are gentle, frank, and straightforward. One of the most wonderful things about Kolakowski's writing is that she delicately weaves science and research in such a way that it doesn't overwhelm the reader. Instead, *When Depression Hurts Your Relationship* empowers, informs, and inspires with hope and encouragement."

—**Deborah Serani, PsyD**, psychologist and award-winning author of *Living with Depression*

"Kolakowski has written a wonderfully practical book to help people dealing with depression and struggling to preserve their relationships. She integrates her psychology expertise in very simple and easy-to-follow ways. From attachment to coping styles, Kolakowski addresses the psychological aspects of depression that contribute to hurting a relationship, and offers practical and easy exercises to break away from harmful patterns. The book is a great resource—not only for people dealing with depression in their relationship, but also for any couple wanting to improve their communication style, add mindfulness in the relationship, and gain sexual intimacy. As a professor and psychologist working with couples, I intend to recommend this book to my psychology students and couples as an easy read and addendum to clinical work."

—**Dinelia Rosa, PhD**, president-elect of the New York State Psychological Association, director of the Dean Hope Center for Educational and Psychological Services at Columbia University, and adjunct associate professor at the clinical psychology program at Teachers College, Columbia University

"Depression is one of the greatest obstacles in relating to others or yourself. *When Depression Hurts Your Relationship* is a wonderful remedy for making sure that this doesn't happen to you or your relationship. It is the right book at the right time, and will help millions of people prevent depression from getting in the way of living happily ever after."

> —**Mark Goulston, MD,** author of *Just Listen: Discover the Secret to Getting Through to Absolutely Anyone*

"If you are depressed, new hope and a new life await, thanks to the book *When Depression Hurts Your Relationship*. In it, you'll find a clear, compassionate, and comprehensive guide, filled with hands-on activities and exercises to steer you through the morass of depression and stagnation that's separating you from your partner. Thanks to Kolakowski's invaluable resource, you can rebuild your connection with your partner to be stronger than ever, and find comfort in each other's arms once again."

> —**Sheri Meyers, PsyD,** licensed marriage and family therapist and author of *Chatting or Cheating: How to Detect Infidelity, Rebuild Love and Affair-Proof Your Relationship*

"In this new book, Shannon Kolakowski shows a deep and compassionate understanding of the ways in which depression shows up in our most cherished relationships. Based on research and Kolakowski's own clinical experience, this book is accessible to real people with real relationship goals. Packed with reflective exercises and concrete tools, *When Depression Hurts Your Relationship* will empower you (and your partner) to create a healthy and loving bond."

—**Heidi Reeder, PhD**, author of *Commit to Win* and associate professor of communication at Boise State University, ID

"*When Depression Hurts Your Relationship* provides readers with scientifically-grounded yet accessible knowledge that they can apply to their lives. It's a valuable contribution to the genre of science-help, and I have no doubt that it will help readers improve their relationships and live more fulfilling lives."

—**David DiSalvo**, author of *Brain Changer: How Harnessing Your Brain's Power to Adapt Can Change Your Life*

when depression hurts your relationship

How to Regain Intimacy and Reconnect with Your Partner When You're Depressed

Shannon Kolakowski, PsyD

New Harbinger Publications, Inc.

To Rob, my husband,
whose love inspires me

Publisher's Note

This publication is designed to provide accurate and authoritative information in regard to the subject matter covered. It is sold with the understanding that the publisher is not engaged in rendering psychological, financial, legal, or other professional services. If expert assistance or counseling is needed, the services of a competent professional should be sought.

Distributed in Canada by Raincoast Books

Copyright © 2014 by Shannon Kolakowski
New Harbinger Publications, Inc.
5674 Shattuck Avenue
Oakland, CA 94609
www.newharbinger.com

Cover design by Amy Shoup; Acquired by Wendy Millstine; Edited by Brady Kahn

Library of Congress Cataloging-in-Publication Data

Kolakowski, Shannon.
 When depression hurts your relationship : how to regain intimacy and reconnect with your partner when you're depressed / Shannon Kolakowski, PsyD.
    pages cm
 Includes bibliographical references.
 ISBN 978-1-60882-832-6 (pbk. : alk. paper) -- ISBN 978-1-60882-833-3 (pdf e-book) -- ISBN 978-1-60882-834-0 (epub) 1. Emotions. 2. Intimacy (Psychology) 3. Man-woman relationships. 4. Self-actualization (Psychology) I. Title.
 BF511.K65 2014
 158.2--dc23
                                    2013050531

Printed in the United States of America

16   15   14

10   9   8   7   6   5   4   3   2   1   First printing

Contents

Acknowledgments vii

Foreword ix

Introduction 1

1 The Uninvited Guest, Depression 11

2 Addressing the Uninvited Guest, Depression 27

3 Managing Painful Emotions 49

4 How to Connect with Your Partner When You're Worried 77

5 How to Feel Good Enough for Your Partner 105

6 Reigniting Your Sexual Desire 125

7 Creating Intimate Understanding 151

Final Thoughts 179

References 181

Acknowledgments

My gratitude goes out to the entire team at New Harbinger Publications. Special thanks to my brilliant editor, Wendy Millstine, for your wisdom, vision, and guidance. Thank you to the outstanding editors Jess Beebe and Nicola Skidmore for your invaluable insight. Thank you to talented freelancer Brady Kahn for adding clarity and precision to the manuscript.

To my family, extended family, colleagues, and friends, thank you for being by my side and lending your understanding, humor, and insight. To my lovely mother: you are a role model and a source of strength to me. To my brother, Ryan, whose sense of humor can make me laugh like no one else can: I'm glad to have you in my life.

With loving memory, I hold gratitude for the wonderful years I had with my father and grandmother. Dad, your loving and inspiring words will always be with me. You always believed in me and instilled in me the confidence to pursue my dreams. To grandmother Margie, my admiration of your grace and elegance remains unparalleled. Thank you for all that you taught me about life and love.

For my clients, thank you for allowing me the privilege of being a part of your lives.

To my husband, Rob, words cannot express how deeply I appreciate you. You've shown me the true meaning of love and intimacy. Thank you for your loving patience, support, encouragement, and unrelenting faith in me. It is because of you that I hold joy, hope, passion, and love in my heart each day.

To all of you who made this book possible: thank you.

Foreword

I've devoted my life to understanding relationships. In a sense, I suppose we all have, simply by virtue of living in them each and every day, but for me it's always been a bit of an obsession. My first published research, for example, was all about relationships—several hundred, in fact—not just how they form, but how the best ones transform us, by sparking dramatic growth in self-esteem and confidence. Over time, as I grew as a clinician, I kept writing and teaching and speaking about relationships whenever and wherever I could—in my workshops and articles, through media interviews, as an instructor at Harvard. And through it all, I developed one consistent message: we can overcome just about anything once we've understood our roles in creating or blocking intimacy with others. Learn how your relationships work, and you've grasped an important key to change.

Dr. Kolakowski clearly shares that point of view. She and I both write columns for *The Huffington Post*, which is where we met; and as we read and shared each other's work, it soon became obvious that we agreed upon a great many things, including the fact that as a culture, our entire approach to depression needs a serious overhaul—namely, by taking people's relationships into account.

Needless to say, we became quick friends.

Up until recently, the field of mental health left relationships out of the discussion, as if problems like depression or anxiety or addiction existed in a realm all their own, mysteriously located outside the hum and buzz of human interaction. In fact, many clinicians thought of depression as a kind of emotional pathogen contracted in early childhood. The cure, from this point of view, was simple: slog through the hard work of therapy, take your medications as prescribed—in privacy, of course; no need to involve one's partner—heal the pains of the past or break out of archaic, misguided beliefs, and, with enough time and patience, the depression would slowly resolve itself.

Except, of course, it didn't. Something far too big was missing.

Most self-help books on depression give at most a simple nod to the fact that people with depression might be in relationships. They might even teach assertiveness tools or help you identify problematic thoughts about the people around you, but they certainly don't examine how depression and relationships shape one another. In that way, they adopt the old view. Just get better, they say. Your relationships will follow.

And that's why we need a book like this. We need it because we can't afford to continue viewing depression as if the cause or cure resides solely in the mind of the person who's depressed. We need it because it matters, deeply, how we behave with others when we're depressed and it matters, just as profoundly, how they respond to us. Depression affects relationships; relationships affect depression. It's a vicious circle. But when its truth is honored, as it is in the pages of this book, the circle becomes a virtuous loop through which we can improve our relationships, and in turn, our relationships can improve us. Our very sense of who we are can be opened up and revised with the right tools. And that revision can help us overcome depression.

That's the inspiring and hopeful message of this book, beginning with the opening chapters, in which readers learn not just the nature of their depression, but how it influences their style of interaction (and vice versa). With each chapter, Dr. Kolakowski systematically builds on this theme, going far beyond symptom management (though she provides plenty of tools for that, as well); she teaches you how protect your relationship when fears, sadness, confusion, shattered self-esteem, and emotional pain threaten to distort and bury your own healthy need for closeness. Then she provides knowledge and skills you need to reconnect sexually and even deepen your intimacy. And she does all this with concrete, practical, research-backed advice, and exercises, both of which draw on decades of relationship research.

In short, *When Depression Hurts Your Relationship* is an important contribution, precisely because it arms you with the tools to take responsibility for your emotional health without ever losing sight of the fact that any work you do—any steps you take to change or grow or simply feel better—can happen only in the context of healthy relationships.

"As much as depression can be a burden on your relationship," Dr. Kolakowski writes in her first chapter, "a good relationship can also be a source of strength and resiliency for you both."

I couldn't agree more.

May you use this book not just to feel better but also to love better.

—Dr. Craig Malkin
　　Instructor of Psychology, Harvard Medical School
　　Director, YM Psychotherapy and Consultation, Inc.
　　Cambridge, MA

Introduction

It's a question I am frequently asked, and one that most of us probably have asked at some point: "Is it normal to have this many problems in our relationship? Do other couples have these kinds of problems?" Yes, and yes—emphatically. Every couple goes through hard times where they struggle to connect.

The very nature of being so close to someone, of loving them and being loved by them, opens you up in a way that not many other situations do. So often, the people we love the most are the ones we have the most problems with. And even though everyone goes through relationship difficulties, when you're in the thick of it, it can feel like you're very much alone.

When you're depressed as well, your relationship problems can seem insurmountable.

Depression sneaks into your thoughts, your feelings, the way you interact with your loved ones. It colors your world with a negative hue—everything seems darker and less hopeful. Depression saps your energy, drains your motivation, and makes it difficult to enjoy time with your partner. When you struggle with it, it becomes difficult to engage in the world around you. You start to have less and less confidence in your partner, in yourself, and in your relationship. You feel lost and overwhelmed, with a sense that things will never get better. When you're depressed, you tend to perceive your partner's interactions more negatively and feel higher levels of guilt and shame, and you are more likely to be overcome in the face of difficult emotions. In essence, you may feel poorly equipped to manage unexpected or emotional events in your relationship.

The other side of the coin is that relationship problems can be a precursor for depression. Large amounts of relationship stress—arguing, anger, resentment, and withdrawal—are difficult for anyone to deal with. But if you've struggled with depression, relationship problems may send you into a downward spiral. Constant conflict that never gets resolved—explosive fights and angry words—makes you want to retreat from your partner. One or both of you may withdraw from the relationship altogether, trying to avoid conflict by keeping your thoughts to yourself. But that doesn't really solve the problem, and you end up feeling disconnected and lonely.

You probably were drawn to this book because, on some level, you know that the warning signs of depression have been there. Trouble engaging with your partner, being self-critical, feeling irritated and let down by your partner. Feeling like he doesn't understand you or wondering what you ever saw in her. As you read this book, you may start to recognize these warning signs even more strongly, and some of them may not fit with what you typically think of as "depression." This book will show you how the pieces fit together and what you can do to help.

For too long, the treatment of depression has been confined to looking at the individual. Yet the research is irrefutable: depression hurts your relationship satisfaction (Davila et al. 1997), and being unhappy in your relationship contributes to depression (Whisman 2001). Depression doesn't stay in a little bubble that encircles only the depressed person; it affects both of you and how you feel about your relationship.

My goal is to help you have a healthy relationship with your partner and with yourself. This book will teach you new ways of thinking about yourself and your relationship. The practical skills offered here are based on years of research. Some of these skills will seem intuitive and some may take you by surprise. Again, the goal here is to encourage you to approach your circumstances in a whole new way.

You and your partner have a bond that no other two people share. This special bond defines your intimacy. If your bond has been damaged by depression, this book will help you rebuild it.

The Meaning of Intimacy

Sometimes the word "intimacy" conjures up images of two people embracing and holding one another with unadulterated adoration. But that's not always how it goes in the real world, is it? Other times, "intimacy" seems like a polite way of saying "sex." While sex and intimacy are closely linked, the concept of intimacy goes beyond sex. Intimacy is the ability to show your partner what's in your heart even when you feel vulnerable and uncertain. It's about letting your partner in, even when it's easier to withdraw or keep fighting. Intimacy is about going through the unpredictable ups and downs of life together while also maintaining your own sense of self. It's the ability to share and soothe and connect. It's the crux of all relationships; a relationship lives or dies by its intimacy.

So how do you gain intimacy? Where does it come from? The bond of intimacy starts developing right when you first meet someone, whether or not you realize it at the time. Think back to when you first met your partner. How did you meet? What were you doing at the time? What did you like about him? How did you know how she felt about you? There was probably a moment, early on, when you recognized that you could be close to your partner. Perhaps it was a flicker of recognition when you told her of an experience, and she said, "Me too." It might have been seeing something of yourself in this other person or having a sense of being familiar and at ease with him. Beyond chemistry or physical attraction, you felt that this other person could really know you.

A good friend of mine came back from her second date with her now-husband. She told me that she had mentioned to him that she'd had a rough day at work. She was ready to brush past it and talk about something else, but then he asked her to tell him about what had happened. In that moment—in his wanting to know more about how she truly felt and in her response—they began to establish a sense of intimacy and closeness.

Attachment researchers have studied love and attachment for decades. The findings overwhelmingly show that partners who consistently seek one another out for comfort and a sense of security report the highest levels of happiness together (Mikulincer and Shaver 2007). Think about the times you've felt the most connected to your partner. Try to recall what you were doing together that made you feel so close to her, when you felt that you were giving your heart and your love freely, when you received her love. What did it feel like? Those moments of connection are what drew you together, and it's moments like these that you can work to create again.

Even when your relationship is in trouble, the bond that you two have formed remains strong. Time may have changed some things: your circumstances or experiences may have shifted, and there might be times when you haven't felt so close. But your bond is always there, in the background, waiting to be revived and celebrated. There are moments every day in your relationship where you can recapture the intimacy that you share. What helps your bond to thrive is nurturing your own sense of self-worth, being a supportive partner, and learning how to break the more destructive patterns of conflict when they arise.

I have worked with many individuals and couples who've come through the lows of depression and are back to feeling fulfilled in their relationships. They were able to recognize that the problem was not their relationships; the problem was how they were in their relationships when depression was present and holding them back. I will share some of their stories with you in this book. You will see how they were able to improve their relationships and their lives as they gained new insight, learned useful skills, and made some practical changes in their interactions with their partners.

I wrote this book for men and women of any age who have experienced depression and have struggled with their romantic relationships. The concepts and exercises are effective for people in all kinds of relationships. Whether you're married or living together, have been together eight months or twenty-eight years, this book will help you. And if you're single, you can use this book to improve your understanding of how depression may have damaged past relationships and to learn what you can do differently in the future.

If you have a depressive disorder (see chapter 1), this book isn't meant to take the place of professional treatment. Instead, the exercises and information presented here will serve as a useful addition to your therapy or couples counseling. The goal of this book is to help you approach your partnership with a healthy attitude and self-awareness that will make your relationship thrive.

How to Use This Book

This book is for the person who is depressed or is having some symptoms of depression. Almost all of the exercises are intended for you to do individually. A few of the exercises may be done with your partner, especially those targeting communication skills. If your partner is unable—or unwilling—to participate in the exercises, that's okay. Positive transformation in relationships often comes from one partner making changes first. As you begin to treat your relationship the way you'd like it to be, you will set the stage for your relationship to become healthy and more fulfilling.

The key is to be patient with yourself and your partner as you begin to make changes. How you're currently approaching your relationship is probably very different from what you'll learn how to do. The good news is that this book contains many helpful guidelines. With some patience, practice, and willingness, you'll be equipped to connect to your partner in a much deeper, more meaningful way.

Within these pages, you'll find answers to the most common problems that people with depression have in relationships. Chapter 1 will help you understand how depression affects your relationship with your loved one. Chapter 2 explains what to do when you're faced with the most common ways depression can hurt your relationship. Chapter 3 will help you identify and cope with upsetting emotions associated with depression and will teach you how to establish a different, more effective style of relating to your partner. Chapter 4 explores the role of worry, rumination, and fear in your relationship and gives you some tools for coping with relationship anxiety. It will help you identify new ways of interacting with your partner to reduce your worry and strengthen your connection.

Chapter 5 will help you explore how self-esteem, identity, and self-acceptance relate to your well-being in your relationship. Chapter 6 will cover how depression can lower your desire for sex, and it will offer some life-changing tools to help you reinvest in and improve your sexual relationship.

Chapter 7 will give you some tools for clearing up misunderstandings, dealing with conflict, and strengthening your bond with your partner. You'll learn several new communication tools, such as how to validate your partner's experience and how to accept differing points of view.

This book is designed to help you move from feeling isolated to feeling like you're on the same team with your partner. The chapters build on each other, so you'll get the most out of reading them sequentially. You may complete some exercises several times or use them on an ongoing basis, while you may choose to skip others. Your partner may want to read this book as well, to better understand what you're going through and how to help. Whatever approach you take, this book is designed to help you do what you can to give your relationship the best chance of success.

Tools and Strategies

The central premise of this book stems from interpersonal therapy (IPT). IPT is based on the notion that depression is often closely tied to social and interpersonal events. We know that genetics and personality, combined with disruptive social events such as the death of a loved one or the loss of a relationship, often contribute to mood disorders (Weissman, Markowitz, and Klerman 2000). IPT is an evidence-based treatment for depression that helps you better cope with life situations that are linked to your current suffering (Markowitz and Weissman 2004).

The main idea behind IPT is that depression is entwined with your relationships. IPT helps you look at what life circumstances may have caused you to become depressed while also looking at what life circumstances are maintaining your depression currently (Klerman et al. 1984). It takes into account your personality and ways you relate to your partner that may be continuing or worsening the cycle of depression. IPT considers your personal history and past experiences, but it is really focused on the here-and-now of your life. The tools in this book cover the following areas:

- Your personality and style of relating to others

- Your symptoms that stem from depression

- Your conflict patterns with your partner

- How painful emotions affect your relationships

- Major changes, loss, transitions, and stressors in your life

- Clarifying your wishes and goals for a satisfying relationship

- Identifying and reinforcing your strengths and assets

This book will help you explore each of these areas. The reason IPT is so effective for depression is that it allows you to alter your perception of your own ability to cope and change. Once you understand the mechanisms that underlie your depression, new choices will become available to you. Rather than being withdrawn and disconnected from your partner, you will learn how to use tools to bring you closer and more in sync with your loved one.

This book also focuses on teaching mindfulness and acceptance. *Mindfulness* is an awareness of your present experience. It's a way of approaching your present moment with an open, nonjudgmental attitude. *Acceptance* means approaching your range of emotions and experiences with curiosity. For couples, this means acknowledging that a range of thoughts and emotions will naturally ebb and flow within any relationship.

Acceptance does not mean embracing pain or resigning yourself to being forever unhappy. Quite the opposite: when you're able to acknowledge the reality of any given situation, there are more opportunities for change. Acceptance allows you to let go of the unrealistic goal of trying to make your relationship free of conflict or in a perpetual state of harmony; the aim is instead to notice the dynamics of your relationship as they happen. You begin to make space for your own range of reactions, thoughts, desires, and wishes, and also to make room for your partner's range of experiences.

Mindfulness and acceptance skills are extremely helpful in managing the distress that comes from depression and difficulties in your relationship. Rather than resist the fear or uncertainty you may experience when your partnership feels unstable, you can learn to explore it, look into it, learn from it, and move past it.

Depression can be painful and lonely to go through, but there is hope. Because depression is such a widespread problem, researchers and clinicians have studied depression in relationships extensively. The tools in this book draw on decades of research and proven interventions that you can learn to implement in your own life.

I wrote this book because I want you to know that there is a way for things to get better for you. You don't have to feel you're doomed to "always have trouble with relationships" or to "always be depressed." What if, instead, you could say, "Even though I sometimes struggle with depression, I have a really strong relationship"? When you're willing to take the time to look inside and examine your relationship, so much can be accomplished. A healthy, loving relationship is possible, despite problems with depression.

chapter 1

The Uninvited Guest, Depression

Claire and Michael were seated in my office on opposite sides of the couch. Michael was well dressed, articulate, and polite. He began by saying that he was worried about Claire, his wife of four years, because of the changes he'd been noticing: she was no longer affectionate, she didn't entertain or invite over friends and family—which he noted that she used to love doing—and she was confiding in him less and less. When they did speak, she was short with him and highly critical. He felt she was a stranger, and he wanted the old Claire back.

Claire's eyes had been downcast the whole time he spoke. She looked up with anguish in her eyes and said, "I don't know why, but I just can't feel close to him. The more he tries to get close to me, the more I push him away! I can't stand feeling like this, but I don't know what to do. What am I supposed to do?" Thus began our work together.

As the sessions went on, Claire became more tearful as she discussed how her depression affected her love for Michael: "I hate that I take it out on him. He doesn't deserve this. But I feel so lost and so upset, and even when he's being nice, it feels like nothing he does is right. And then I start feeling guilty for treating him so badly. It makes it worse, and I realize I'm not good enough for him. I don't know why he stays with me."

Michael and Claire are a couple whose relationship has been hurt by an uninvited guest named depression. Neither of them knew that Claire was struggling with depression, but through our work in therapy, we identified certain moments in their relationship that marked her descent into a depressive episode. We also found that Claire had struggled with some depression symptoms as a teenager and had a family history of relationship problems.

Over time, Claire began to connect more to her emotions and to Michael. She was able to work through some of the sadness that had been present for quite some time. Once we identified the problem of depression and how the relationship was being hurt, Claire and Michael were able to begin making some changes to help their relationship handle the uninvited guest.

If you are like Claire, depression diminishes your ability to connect with and enjoy the person you love. You begin to criticize yourself and your partner and to doubt your relationship altogether. It's so discouraging when nothing feels right. You may lose interest in sex, feel disconnected, and feel exhausted. Painful feelings of isolation, worthlessness, and hopelessness can make it hard to trust your own instincts. Irritability and anger drive a wedge between you and your partner. Your past haunts you, and you worry about the future. As you deal with your own sadness, your connection with your partner seems to be slipping away.

It's sometimes hard to fully recognize depression; this uninvited guest doesn't come with a name tag. This chapter will help you understand the problems you're having that are related to depression and show you how to transform the uninvited guest into something less intimidating.

Identifying the Symptoms of Depression

Depression is a complex disorder, but there are three general areas to look at when evaluating if you may be depressed. The main focus should be on changes in how you are feeling, thinking, and behaving.

Changes in Mood

First, you may notice changes in your *mood*. Perhaps you felt, and still feel, deeply sad, as if the sadness overwhelms any possibility of feeling happy or hopeful. With this sadness, you may experience tears and crying on a daily basis. You may notice that it doesn't take much to irritate or annoy you—your emotional threshold feels low, even when you're really making an effort. You may have angry outbursts, lack patience, and feel "on edge."

Another way that your emotions may be affected by depression is in the form of feeling numb, or devoid of emotions. You may notice that you don't feel anything at all. You don't feel sad. You don't feel happy. You just feel hollow. Emotions have been replaced by a sense of emptiness; you are unable to feel emotions even when you try to feel something.

Any of these changes in mood—a deep sense of sadness, agitation or moodiness, or a sense of numbness or emptiness—can be symptoms of depression and may signal that depression is present.

Changes in Thinking

Next, you may notice changes in your *thinking*. Depression is characterized by overly negative, critical, or hopeless thoughts. This means that it's hard to see the glass half-full. One of the best descriptions of how depression affects your thoughts comes from cognitive therapist Aaron Beck. Depression is characterized by what Beck calls a cognitive triad—negative thoughts about yourself, a negative outlook on the world, and a pessimistic view of the future (Beck et al. 1979). Indeed, when my clients describe feeling discouraged and hopeless, it is often the idea that things will never get better that is most upsetting. It's the sense of dread about the future that really feels so discouraging.

You may notice your thoughts about yourself are derogatory.

- *I'm always messing up at work. I'm a failure.*

- *I ruined another date night. There's something about me that is unlovable, broken.*

- *I'm worthless and mean. My family would be better off without me.*

Your thoughts about others may tend to be harsh.

- *She can't possibly understand me.*

- *Other people have it so easy in life.*

- *People always look for the worst in each other. I bet he's noticing my faults.*

Ominous, negative thoughts about the future are prevalent.

- *I'll never really be happy. Something always goes wrong.*

- *What's the point of learning about this? Nothing ever helps.*

- *The future will only bring more pain.*

As such, it is difficult to simply "cheer up" and "look on the bright side," as well-meaning friends or family may suggest. It feels instead like there is no bright side. Your thoughts may automatically reject signs of hope as a way to protect yourself from being disappointed, searching instead for confirmation of how desperate things feel inside.

Changes in Behavior

Lastly, changes in your recent *behavior* can serve as indicators of depression. You may notice that you have less desire to be active or to do hobbies that you used to enjoy. It's too much effort to even think about doing something. You may have trouble being around others and prefer to be alone. You may find yourself drinking more or using drugs to help you escape or to dull your feelings. You likely have trouble concentrating, have trouble getting your work done, or find that you lack motivation. Often people experience changes in their sleep patterns—it may be hard to get to sleep, or you may end up sleeping for really long periods of time. All of these changes in your behavior are signals that depression may be present.

Sometimes your friends or family members will be the ones to point out these changes: "You never come to the games with me anymore," "You seem to be drinking a lot lately," or "You always seem angry." While this feedback may be difficult to hear, it often comes from family members or friends who care about you but are unsure of how to help you. Listening to their feedback with openness is a good first step to take.

Types of Depression

Depressive disorders vary based on your symptoms and how long you've had them. Not everyone who has symptoms of depression has a depressive disorder. In fact, most people feel low or struggle from time to time, and this is a normal part of living your life. You may recognize some of the mood symptoms listed as criteria for a depressive disorder without meeting all the criteria for that disorder.

Major Depressive Disorder

Major depressive disorder (MDD) is a type of depression defined by one or more episodes of major depression. With a major depressive episode, changes in your mood, thinking, and behavior end up causing problems with significant others or make it hard for you to keep up your daily routine. How many of the following symptoms have you felt daily for the past two weeks? How about other periods in your past?

- Depressed mood most of the day, nearly every day

- Agitation, restlessness, and irritability

- Changes in appetite, often losing or gaining weight without meaning to

- Difficulty concentrating

- Fatigue and lack of energy

- Feeling hopeless and helpless

- Feelings of worthlessness, self-loathing, and guilt

- Becoming withdrawn or isolated from others

- Loss of interest or pleasure in activities you once enjoyed

- Thoughts of death, suicide, or harming yourself

- Trouble sleeping at night or excessive sleeping

Having five or more of these symptoms every day for at least a two-week period, which interferes with your work, education, relationship, or daily functioning, is the standard criterion for a major depressive episode (American Psychiatric Association 2013).

Dysthymic Disorder

Dysthymia is a persistent low-level depression. With dysthymia, you'll notice a low mood present nearly every day for at least two years. Dysthymic disorder doesn't have the full force of a major depressive episode. Instead, it's a general, ever-present feeling of disinterest and hopelessness. In addition to chronic low mood, you would experience two or more of the following (American Psychiatric Association 2013):

- Poor appetite or overeating

- Insomnia or sleeping too much

- Low energy or fatigue

- Low self-esteem

- Poor concentration or difficulty making decisions

- Feelings of hopelessness

If you have dysthymia, you may look back and have trouble remembering a time when you didn't feel down.

Seasonal Affective Disorder

Seasonal affective disorder (SAD) is a type of depression that follows a seasonal pattern. The most common pattern for SAD includes an onset of depression and negative thinking beginning in the fall, with a continuation of symptoms throughout winter, and symptoms decreasing in the spring. With SAD, you'll notice daytime sleepiness, carbohydrate cravings, and overeating (Partonen and Pandi-Perumal 2009). Biological reactions to lack of sunlight and vitamin D are thought to cause this type of depression.

Double Depression

Double depression is when you have both MDD and dysthymic disorder. It's diagnosed when you've had an episode of major depression that occurs at least two years after you develop dysthymic disorder. Studies find that over 75 percent of people with dysthymic disorder will experience double depression at some point in their lives (Klein and Santiago 2003). Researchers are still in the process of identifying if major depression and dysthymia are two separate disorders that share common features or if dysthymia is a precursor to major depression.

How Depression Develops

If you had your first experience of depression as a teenager, you are not alone. The uninvited guest, depression, usually emerges on the scene in your teens or early adulthood. It's estimated that 20 percent of adolescents will have had a depressive disorder by the time they're eighteen years old. In any given year, 2 percent of kids and 4 to 7 percent of teens will struggle with depression (Beardslee, Gladstone, and O'Conner 2012). In adulthood, nearly one in five people will be diagnosed with a depressive disorder in their lifetimes (Kessler et al. 2005).

Why do some people struggle with depression while others do not? Research suggests that depression develops in two different ways.

Biology

A family history of mood disorders means that you may be more likely to have a genetic predisposition to depression. Naturally occurring chemicals found in the body, called neurotransmitters, have been found to relate to depression; these include serotonin, dopamine, norepinephrine, glutamate, and gamma-Aminobutyric acid (GABA). Changes in hormones also play a large role in depression, including problems with thyroid. For women, hormone changes occur during puberty, during pregnancy, during the premenstrual cycle, and during menopause. Because of the role of hormones and physiology, if you are experiencing a depressed mood, you should see your doctor to rule out any physical or medical causes.

Environment

The other pathway to the development of depression includes your social surroundings and your life history. People who have been maltreated or who were physically, emotionally, or sexually abused in childhood are at a much higher risk of developing depression. Early mistreatment leads to the development of an overactive stress response and also results in negative, self-defeating thought patterns.

The particular interaction of these two pathways, or how biology meets environment in certain psychological disorders, is usually called the stress-diathesis hypothesis. This hypothesis takes into account each person's specific vulnerabilities for developing depression (Brown and Harris 1989). Negative life events or stressors—such as the death of a loved one or a separation ending a relationship—can activate your depression. In fact, 80 percent of people who experience depression have undergone recent stressful life events (Kessler 1997). But not everyone who experiences a stressful life event develops depression. Why is that?

To account for these differences, the stress-diathesis hypothesis contends that the more genetically predisposed to depression you are, the less severe your life stressors need be for your depression to become activated. If someone were less vulnerable to depression, it would take more environmental stress for him to develop depression. For instance, two people could both experience a divorce, and the person who is more biologically vulnerable to depression would respond with depression and have greater difficulty coping, whereas a different person with no depressive predisposition could experience the same situation—or an even nastier divorce—without having a depressive reaction.

Since depression tends to occur as a downward cycle, the depression symptoms you experience can cause you to feel hopeless and helpless, thus making your symptoms worse. Once you've had one depressive episode, you're at an increased risk for having episodes of depression in the future (Monroe 2010).

Gender Differences in Depression

Men and women are different in many ways, and the uninvited guest, depression often shows up differently depending on your gender.

While both men and women may experience depression after a disruption in a close relationship, such as a breakup or separation, women may have a higher vulnerability and reactivity to these stressful life events, causing depression in younger women in particular (Nolen-Hoeksema and Jackson 2001). Women are more likely to internalize their depression. Internalization means that you pull your sadness inward and take on depression as a reflection of negative beliefs about your inner self. You're likely to ruminate, meaning that you think about the same worry or idea over and over again. You end up feeling lonely, isolated, and painfully aware of your inner feelings.

Conversely, men are more likely than women to externalize their depression (Eaton et al. 2012). If you're a man, this means your depression may come out through such behaviors as drinking alcohol, becoming aggressive, seeking extramarital affairs, or withdrawing from your loved ones. You're likely to have physical symptoms, such as backaches, and problems with low sexual desire. As a man, you are also less likely than a woman to identify your symptoms as depression and are less likely to seek help or treatment (Davidson and Meltzer-Brody 1999). And society doesn't do a great job of recognizing your depression either; research indicates that physicians are more likely to miss a diagnosis of depression in men, and people in general are more likely to overlook the warning signs of depression in men (Swami 2012).

Knowing about these gender differences gives you a great advantage in fighting depression. The sooner you recognize your symptoms as depression, the better. Research indicates that when one partner is depressed, there is a greater likelihood that the other partner will become depressed (Gadassi, Mor, and Rafaeli 2011). Because of this, it's important to be able to recognize signs of depression in yourself and in your partner. Understanding is an essential first tool as you start on the path of healing.

Love and Depression

The research is resounding. There is a strong correlation between depression and marital dissatisfaction (Goldfarb et al. 2007). The connection goes both ways: depression tends to hurt your relationship satisfaction, and being unhappy in your relationship contributes to depression.

When you're depressed, it's hard to see your own surroundings clearly. The primary feature of depression is distortion, meaning your perception of your life—including your relationship—is easily warped and represented in a more negative way. You may find yourself having more and more negative thoughts about your partner and your relationship with each other.

As you saw in the example of Michael and Claire, sometimes depression hurts relationships without either partner being aware of what a large role depression is playing. By closely examining your recent feelings, thoughts, and behaviors, you can examine whether or not depression is hurting your own relationship.

Exercise: Is Depression Hurting Your Relationship?

To establish if depression is affecting your relationship, think back and answer these questions about your experiences over the past several months.

	Yes	No
Do you find you are frequently agitated or irritable?		
Does your partner describe you as moody?		
Do you constantly seek reassurance from your partner?		
Has your sex drive decreased?		
Do you find yourself feeling guilty or worried about how your mood affects your partner?		
Have you had trouble sleeping?		
Do you secretly worry that your partner will leave you for someone better?		
Do you and your partner disagree more and more often about what you will do together as a couple?		
Have you lost interest in activities that you and your partner once enjoyed doing together?		
Do you sometimes feel unworthy of your partner despite your partner's reassurance that you're the one he or she wants to be with?		
Do you have trouble concentrating on conversations with your partner or paying attention to the details of your partner's day?		

Do you feel restless or bored when you are with your partner, regardless of what you are doing?		
Have you experienced a significant increase or decrease in weight without having intended to change your weight?		
Do you have trouble making plans for the future?		
Do you tend to focus on the negative aspects of yourself?		
Do you tend to criticize your partner, focusing on his or her flaws?		
Have you increased your alcohol intake?		
Have you noticed an increase in angry outbursts?		
Do you feel less able to deal with stress in your relationship?		
Do you find yourself withdrawing from your partner to avoid conflict?		
Do you find yourself leaning more and more on your partner to do the housework, take care of the kids, or make the decisions and plans for your social life?		
Do you find yourself less able to relate to your partner's concerns or difficult emotions?		

Total Total

If you answered yes to five or more of these questions, it is likely that depression is hurting your relationship with your loved one. The good news is you can do something about it. Since depression can cause you to perceive your relationship in a negative light, and since relationship problems can increase depression, you can begin by working on either end—the perception or the reality—to transform the cycle.

You may feel ashamed or guilty about your struggle with depression. Helping you deal with painful emotions such as shame and guilt is one of the main focuses of this book, because these emotions are so prevalent in depression. Future chapters will discuss some ways to cope with these feelings. For now, however, you deserve credit for having the courage to take this step of looking deeper within yourself.

The truth is, you didn't choose to feel this way, and you didn't do anything to deserve feeling so low. Rarely do people set out with the goal of having depression harm their relationships. Yes, we have all made mistakes, hurt the people we love, and behaved in ways that we wish we could take back. That is part of what makes us human. But failing to forgive yourself and taking away the possibility of happiness will not help anyone involved. This is your chance to become the kind of loving partner that you long to be.

Relationships as Support

As much as depression can be a burden on your relationship, a good relationship can also be a source of strength and resiliency for you both (Proulx, Buehler, and Helms 2009). There's evidence that having a strong relationship can reduce your relapse rate from depression, serve as a buffer against negative events, and help individual treatment succeed (Jacobson et al. 1993). To turn your relationship into a support system, you must first understand how it's currently working.

Exercise: Taking a Relationship Inventory

Look at your current relationship, its strengths as well as weaknesses, and consider how both you and your partner are in the relationship. With pen and paper or using your computer, write down the answers to these questions.

- To what degree do you feel emotionally healthy and balanced right now? It may be helpful to use a rating scale of 1 to 10, where 1 represents very unhealthy and 10 represents very healthy and balanced.

- What are your current stressors in life? Name any stressors that you can think of.

- What are the greatest strengths and assets you bring to your relationship? You might say something like, "My greatest strengths are my kindness, my ability to listen well, my ability to problem-solve…" or anything positive about yourself that comes to mind.

- List two examples of when your relationship has felt healthy, loving, and reciprocal. Your examples can be from the past or present time.

- List two recent examples of when your relationship felt the most strained. Elaborate on each example in detail. What led up to the incident? How did you feel, and what did you say and do during the incident? What did you partner say and do? How did you feel and what did you say and do afterward? What did you partner say and do afterward? Are there any patterns evident?

- What's worked well in reducing strain on your relationship? How have you solved problems? What has not worked well?

- What might be preventing you from fully giving your love to your partner right now? What makes you least likely to feel loving toward your partner?

- What might be preventing you from fully receiving your partner's love right now? What makes you least likely to be receptive to receiving your partner's love?

- Which behaviors of yours are most hurtful to your partner? What actions hurt your relationship?

- Which behaviors from your partner are most hurtful to you? When do you feel most hurt?

- Which of the things that you do contributes the most to your relationship's well-being? Name one or two of the best things you can do for your relationship.

- What are your wishes and goals for your relationship? What would make your relationship more satisfying?

- What do you value most, and do you want to continue, in your relationship?

Keep this series of questions and answers for later reference.

If you had trouble answering some of these questions, it's okay. The information and the exercises in this book are meant to help you become better at answering them. You can use your answers to this series of questions as a benchmark as you read on and begin to gain some relief from your struggle to understand your relationship problems. You'll learn new ways to understand your feelings of rejection, problems you have relating to your partner, and the strong sense of loneliness or emptiness that you may feel.

After each chapter, return to this exercise and take another relationship inventory. How have your answers to the questions shifted? What new insights have you gained? It's likely that you'll find yourself answering the questions differently. Seeing your own progress can be exciting, and it will add to your growing sense of confidence and strength. It's a powerful antidote to depression.

Conclusion

This chapter has outlined the basics about depression: how it develops, what it feels like, and how it might play out in your relationship. In taking inventory, you have begun to look more closely at what is helping and what is hurting your relationship.

The next chapter delves into the specifics of how depression enters into relationships and will guide you in making significant improvements in life with your partner. As you read on, ask yourself which forms of this uninvited guest most resonate with you? And, with this new knowledge, what changes can you begin to make today?

chapter 2

Addressing the Uninvited Guest, Depression

This chapter will talk about how depression hurts your relationship when it appears in the form of self-doubt, criticism, focusing on the past, unrealistic standards or expectations, hostility, or insecure attachment. You will see how depression may affect your partnership on a day-to-day basis, and you will begin to make some important changes:

- Finding strength and compassion for yourself amidst self-doubts

- Resolving past issues that affect your current relationship

- Feeling more secure in your relationship

- Feeling more compassionate and loving toward your partner

- Embracing your partner's positive traits

- Beginning to engage and share with your partner more

- Beginning to see hope for your future together

- Holding realistic expectations for your partner

- Having a team mentality when arguments start to get in the way of intimacy

These changes will build a more secure foundation for your relationship, and make it clear that the uninvited guest, depression, is not welcome here.

Depression in the Form of Self-Doubt

"My partner brings out the best in me." It's a common saying, and in many ways it can be true. In a good partnership, your partner will often bring out your best qualities. We're initially drawn to our partners because we feel good about who we are when we're with them. Around him, you feel humorous, attractive, smart, and loving. Around her, you're witty, handsome, more kind and gentle.

But sometimes our loved ones bring out our worst sides. Self-doubt doesn't go away in the presence of people we love or who are amazing. Quite the contrary. When you're depressed, the one you love can activate feelings of self-doubt. People with lower self-esteem tend to perceive their relationships as more fragile and tend to expect their partners to have a lower estimation of them. Someone with lower self-esteem and depression may have a bad time with her partner and think, *She doesn't really care about me. I knew it wouldn't last*, whereas someone with a healthier sense of self-worth may think, *Right now, we're going through a tough time, but I know our relationship can withstand this. We'll work it out*. What this means is that what you bring to the relationship will ultimately have a huge effect on how good you feel in the relationship.

Turning It Around

The best way to be fulfilled and secure within your relationship, then, is to be fulfilled within yourself.

Find Self-Compassion

Self-compassion is a powerful tool, useful both for dealing with depression and living a life of meaning. Having self-compassion means being able to have empathy, concern, and genuine care for yourself. Self-doubt will run you down. It's the voice inside telling you that you're defective, worthless, selfish, or failing. Self-compassion fosters the voice inside of you that says, *It's okay to have failures, setbacks, and to be disappointed. It's part of the human condition. Everyone feels this way sometimes.* Self-compassion is finding patience for flaws in yourself. It's the caring and tender voice that each of us needs to thrive. One way to spot self-doubt is to ask yourself, *Would I speak to a friend the way I speak to myself?* If the answer is no, gently remind yourself to practice kindness and compassion toward yourself. The better you're able to handle your inner critic, the less self-doubt will dictate how you feel about your relationship.

Challenge Your Doubts

Self-doubt can make you feel hopeless, like you have to sit back and take whatever life brings you. Self-doubt tends to be paralyzing, stunting your ability to make changes. To counter this tendency, look for evidence that is contrary to your doubts. What are some times you've felt empowered? Conquered adversity? Look for small ways to affirm that you are capable of affecting your path in life.

Take Action

Doing things to show that you're in control and taking responsibility for your situation is an antidote to self-doubt. Identify one thing you can do right now to make yourself feel better, and do it. Something as simple as cleaning out your car or going for a walk can symbolize your choice to be in charge. Find ways to make daily affirmations that you are in charge of your own life and destiny. As you build your self-confidence, you will see those positive feelings about yourself mirrored in the love you are able to give to and receive from your partner.

Depression in the Form of Criticism

Depression tends to make negative things appear large and looming while minimizing or dismissing the good things in life. You may clearly see all of the negative traits about your partner while missing the positives. As you struggle with depression, this focus on your partner's negative traits may come out in harsh or overly critical thoughts. This critical way of thinking is important to be aware of, as it can quickly derail relationships. Your partner may feel like she's walking on eggshells, unsure of how to approach you, fearful of being criticized.

For example, my client Marcia found that when she's more depressed, it becomes very difficult to deal with her husband leaving clothes or dishes around the house. Any sort of mess she finds causes her to feel extremely irritated, and she finds herself thinking, *He is so inconsiderate! He leaves things all over, and he knows it bugs me. He is selfish!* When Marcia makes an effort to notice the positive traits in her husband —rather than only the negative—she is able to make a more realistic assessment: *He sometimes leaves clutter around the house, which bugs me way more than it bothers him. He also is caring and considerate most of the time, like when he offers to help my mother go to the store and buy groceries or when we decide to go to the movies and he's happy to see whatever film I pick.* Marcia is able to see that her partner has flaws but these flaws don't cancel out his caring traits.

Turning It Around

To combat your tendency to sometimes be overly critical or harsh when you are feeling down, this next exercise will help you to identify your partner's strengths. When you keep your partner's positive attributes at the forefront of your mind, it's easier to appreciate him.

Exercise: Focusing on the Positive

First, make a list of five to seven positive traits your partner holds.

Example: *Janelle is humorous and she makes me laugh*

Next, identify behaviors or ways in which you can actively show appreciation for your partner's strength.

Example: *I can show my appreciation by*

- *Making an effort to make her laugh in return*
- *Thanking her for putting a smile on my face*
- *Complimenting her sense of humor to others in his presence*

Keep this list handy. Remind yourself to reread it, and add to it every week.

Practicing thankfulness for your relationship and for your partner is a proven way to increase your feelings of positive regard. Holding positive regard for your partner is one of the biggest predictors of relationship success (Gottman and Silver 1999). This is because positive regard begets more positive regard. In other words, when your partner feels appreciated, she is much more likely to feel valued and secure and be able to praise your strengths in return.

Depression in the Form of Past Hurt

Another way that depression can prevent you from being close to your partner is by keeping you focused on the past.

In many ways, it's an asset that you are able to look back on painful experiences and learn lessons from them. You learn about how you are resilient, how you can make it through difficulties, and what not to do in the future. Experiencing a bad breakup or seeing your parents get divorced may teach you a lot about how you want to conduct your relationships. You may think, *I never want to fight the way my parents did.* Or you may say to yourself, *Veronica was always putting me down and controlling me. Breaking up with her taught me that I need a girlfriend who is supportive and respectful.* But the adaptive function of looking back on your past can lose its value after a while; with rumination, there is a point of diminishing returns.

Your past can start interfering with your present when you constantly worry about repeating past mistakes or fear that you will be hurt again. You may have unresolved pain from seeing parents or loved ones break up. It may be hard for you to trust another person. You may tend to focus on painful past events and attribute this pain to your current relationship.

The best way to move forward is to understand how your past affects you now and to clearly separate the past from the present. This next exercise will help you identify how past relationship patterns might be influencing your current relationship.

Exercise: Identifying Past Hurts

Make a list of all of your significant relationships with former partners. Include this information about each relationship:

- How long did your relationship last?

- Looking back, what were the events or incidents that damaged your relationship?

- When did these damaging events start happening in your relationship? Right away? Was it two months into the relationship? A year? Later?

- What were the key emotions that you felt with each event?

Once you identify how you were hurt in your past relationships, the next step is to look for themes, or patterns. Have you had more than one relationship in which deceit or betrayal was an issue or where your temper caused conflict? Have previous partners expressed common concerns about you? Also look at time frames. Do you tend to have problems in the wintertime? This might be related to seasonal depression or to some difficulty you have during the holidays. Now examine whether any of these patterns are present in your current relationship.

By evaluating what happened in the past—what previous partners did that may have been wounding, or ways in which you may have hurt them—you can identify what may be triggers, or trouble spots, for you in the present.

For example, Vanessa and Micah were together for two years. Looking back in our sessions together, Vanessa recognized that the relationship was damaged beyond repair one year into their relationship when she found out about Micah's infidelity while away on a business trip. The primary emotions she felt were betrayal and loss of trust. After a year of trying to work past the loss of trust and not succeeding, Micah and Vanessa ended the relationship.

Currently, Vanessa is in a relationship with a man named Samuel. While Samuel has always been faithful and honest, Vanessa struggles with trust, and she worries about betrayal. She tends to become easily upset by small incidents with Samuel that trigger her worry or fear, such as when he is away for the weekend or when she doesn't know exactly what time he will be home. By identifying these tendencies, she can recognize when her past is hurting her current relationship.

Turning It Around

Rather than repeat past patterns of hurt, make an effort to be aware of your triggers. Take a look at how you can break your patterns.

Break the Pattern

If you tend to have difficulties around the holidays, let your partner know that you are going to make an effort this year to treat her with kindness. Make a list of ways that you can take care of yourself, such as taking enough time off of work for travel, making sure you get enough sleep, or watching your alcohol intake. If you have difficulties with trust, make an effort to focus on all of the ways that your partner has proven to be trustworthy.

Stay in the Moment

Because you struggle with depression, it's likely that you tend to ruminate on your fears. If you are getting stuck on unfounded feelings of insecurity, catch yourself by bringing awareness to the here-and-now moment. Ask yourself, *Is this an old feeling coming up? Are these thoughts helping or hurting my relationship right now?* Gently remind yourself of your partner's actual traits when you have suspicions that are unfounded and rooted in past hurts.

Depression in the Form of Unrealistic Standards

Having high standards and high expectations in a relationship is a really good thing. When you expect a lot of your relationship, it means that you're unwilling to settle for one that's subpar. Being devoted to having a fulfilling relationship means that you're willing to work to make things really good. This is an excellent way to approach your love life.

Where things can get tricky is when you have unrealistic expectations about how exactly the relationship will go and how your partner should behave in the relationship. High expectations are good, but impossibly high or rigid expectations are not. It's easy to fall into the trap of assuming your partner knows what you're thinking, knows the right thing to do in any given circumstance, knows when to do it, and knows why he is doing it. Whether you have high expectations about how a family trip will go or about what constitutes a romantic date on Valentine's Day, being too rigid can cause problems.

You may have developed an internal script that dictates what you believe is the ideal way to handle a situation or the optimal way to behave in a relationship. The problem is that your partner hasn't read your script. She may have different ideas too. And of course, life doesn't always go according to how you plan it. For example, my client Thomas was spending the holidays with his girlfriend Ava's family in Vermont for two weeks. Because Ava and he were becoming serious in their relationship, Thomas really wanted the trip to go well. In his script, he pictured himself with Ava's dad and brothers bonding over fishing and football, laughing at the same jokes, connecting through their mutual love for Ava.

The actual trip went fairly well, but the reality wasn't very much like Thomas's script. He'd imagined that Ava's father would be outgoing and humorous but instead found him to be quiet and reserved. Whenever Ava's dad was quiet, Thomas worried that he'd made a mistake or said something to offend him. While Ava's family genuinely liked and embraced Thomas, he was certain they didn't like him, because they hadn't gotten along the way he'd pictured in his script. Since things hadn't played out as he'd imagined, Thomas ended up being disappointed and behaving in a less outgoing manner toward Ava's family.

Thomas's expectations caused him to feel unduly rejected, which affected the way he acted toward Ava's family. Whether it's your partner, your in-laws, or a coworker, when you anticipate how others will act according to your secret script, you are setting the stage for disappointment. When the other person inevitably deviates from your script, the depressed part of you may react with dissatisfaction, disenchantment, or feelings of failure.

Holding impossibly high standards has to do with how you feel about yourself. People who are depressed often have high expectations of themselves and are sensitive to any deviation. For instance, you might expect a certain standard of work to be produced, at a certain level of quality and speed that you've set for yourself. If you don't meet that expectation, you beat yourself up. Similarly, you might have some rigid expectations of your partner—such as that she'll automatically know the right thing to say when you're upset or that he'll react in a particular way to the news you tell him. When your partner fails to comply with your internal script or expectation, you may become disappointed and tell yourself, *If he really cared about me, he would've known what I wanted to hear.* You may attribute your partner's failure to read your mind as a failure in caring when in actuality your partner cares very much about you and may have responded in the best way he knew how. Your partner can't read your mind—no matter how well he knows you—and you may need to be more direct in expressing your needs.

Turning It Around

The antidote to unrealistic expectations is to increase your flexibility in how you approach your interactions.

Nobody's a Mind Reader

Remind yourself that your partner is no mind reader, and she can't magically know what you need or desire. While imagining that our loved ones "just know" how to make us happy may seem romantic, the truth is that most of us need a little help. It doesn't make your love any less strong or amazing if you clue your partner into your needs.

Open Up to Possibility

Another part of having flexibility means being able to recognize that though your ideal scenarios may not always come to fruition, the outcomes can still be a good. Maybe you pictured having a romantic dinner outside gazing at the stars, but the reality was that it rained and you both ended up soaking wet and freezing. This is a turning point. Do you call it a night, reacting with disappointment and defeat? Or do you make the best of it? If you're open to what life brings, the two of you may end up eating inside in front of a roaring fire, laughing and playing a game, and having an even better time than you'd imagined.

Communicate with Your Partner

It's also vital to recognize that just because you have a clear picture of how things should go, it doesn't mean that your partner necessarily has the same idea in mind. Your partner may approach an upcoming vacation with no preconceived notions about how you will spend your time together. You may arrive to your destination, however, already having fully planned out your itinerary. When your partner wants to spend the first day lounging by the pool, it may upset the plans you've designed for the trip. Since expectations are often different, it helps to communicate what you want, listen to the other person's needs, and be willing to compromise.

Exercise: Increasing Flexibility

To increase your flexibility, take the following steps:

First, identify your internal script. What are some instances when you've had an internal script and things turned out differently from your expectations? In your script, what were you hoping would happen? What led you to form this expectation?

Next, look for alternative scenarios. See if you can look at what you were expecting as just one of many ways that things could turn out.

If your script involved expectations of your partner that differed from your partner's own expectations, try to see the situation from your partner's point of view. What might your partner have been thinking in a given situation? If you aren't sure, ask.

Next, focus on the core of why having a different outcome from the script upsets you. What happens if things don't go according to how you envisioned? Do you feel let down? Embarrassed? Annoyed? Could letting go of control make you feel nervous or uncertain? Without judging yourself, try to explore what might have been happening that made the event so important to you.

Consider how you would want to handle similar situations in the future. You can use one the following coping skills to help counter a tendency to have fixed expectations:

- Acknowledge that relationships involve two people who are human and who may have very different needs. There's no one right way to act, feel, think, or be in any given situation.

- Decide to accept your partner's behavior. Work on being okay with the way your partner does things or how an event turns out.

- Make a request for a different behavior. Let your partner know ahead of time what you're hoping for and why it means a lot to you.

- Try to catch yourself when you are developing a detailed or rigid script. Rather than finishing the script, consider some other possibilities and various uncertainties in the situation.

As you examine your internal scripts, challenge yourself to see different outcomes in a new light. Just because you expect one outcome doesn't mean another one is bad. Find the benefits of being open to new experiences.

Being more flexible will help you appreciate what you have in your relationship and in other parts of your life.

This was true in Thomas's case. Once Thomas let go of how he thought things should be, he made room for the reality of how things really were. He ended up developing a really strong relationship with Ava's father that was even deeper than he had hoped for. And he learned that sometimes the best things in life are what you haven't expected or anticipated.

Depression in the Form of Hostility

Challenging each other is a vital part of a healthy relationship. Being equals means that you both will have opinions, and sometimes those opinions will vary. Having a different point of view can make your relationship exciting and passionate. After all, if you agreed on everything all the time, life would be boring.

But have you ever noticed how "friendly" challenges can quickly turn into *I'm right, your wrong, and I'm going to prove to you that I'm right?* When you and your partner don't see eye to eye on an issue, it's fertile ground for a power struggle to emerge. So often it becomes more about being right and winning than resolving the problem. After all, doesn't it feel good to be right? Of course it does! The problem is that being right often comes at a price. The price is harmony and unity, because you and your partner start to see each other as foes, as opposed to partners on the same team. There's not a whole lot of unity in getting the last word.

Depression can make you more irritable and prone to being combative. A pattern of hostility often becomes regular with couples when a partner is depressed, and things can quickly turn nasty. You may criticize your partner during an argument in order to diminish his point of view and prove your point. Then he'll criticize you in return. It becomes a battle of criticism with the winner as the last person standing. This usually happens because it seems that if you can knock down your partner's point of view, you'll win the argument. But again, this kind of exchange doesn't help you feel connected.

Turning It Around

When you notice criticism and hostility emerging, consider these ways to help you break the cycle of hostility.

Get on the Same Team

When you find yourself escalating in an argument with your partner, it can be helpful to say something to break the momentum. Try saying, "I feel like we're attacking each other. I want us to be on the same team. Let's try to work together, so we both can be okay with the outcome. It's not worth it to hurt each other."

Celebrate the Victories

When the two of you accomplish something together—it might be as simple as finishing some yard work or successfully getting your kids tucked into bed—celebrate as a team. The more you use the language of "we" and "team," the more you'll be reminded that you are on the same side.

Consider an Outsider's Perspective

When both you and your partner have a major disparity in how you see something, it can be really helpful to ask yourself, *What would a neutral, outside party have to say?* Imagine that this outsider is altruistic and wants only the best for your family. Try to think about the disagreement from this neutral perspective. What wisdom can you find in what each of you is saying? What potential compromise could be reached by meeting in the middle? If you regularly employ this technique—thinking about problems from a neutral perspective—conflict will decrease, you'll have less distress, and your relationship will benefit.

Recognize the Greater Cause

It also helps to ask yourself, *What's the end goal we're hoping to accomplish?* This allows you to step away from the current dispute to figure out the greater meaning in what you're trying to resolve. By asking this question, you're also acknowledging that you're on the same team with your partner. When you remind yourself of your larger goals, such as having a secure relationship or spending more quality time with your partner, you're able to put the current problem into perspective. Often, you'll find that what you're arguing about doesn't have a great bearing on these larger relationship goals. You may be able to talk to your partner about what your larger relationship goals are and enlist your partner's help. You might say, "We're not seeing eye to eye on this. The most important thing for me is that you and I have a strong relationship. How can we resolve this so that we can get back on track?" Seeing the bigger picture can often help you and your partner look at your current problem in a new light.

Give Yourself Permission to Disagree

Sometimes there's an unspoken rule that the two of you should reach a conclusion about your differences of opinions, or declare a winner. You felt the movie last night was moving and deep, while he found it boring and predictable. It can be fun to discuss the movie and make your case for your perspective, especially if you recognize that ultimately it's okay for you and your partner to feel differently. Sometimes being part of the same team means realizing that you won't always agree. Many arguments can be solved when each of you accepts that *I have my opinion, you have yours. Neither is necessarily wrong or right; they're just different. And I respect—and encourage—our rights to feel differently!*

Depression in the Form of Insecure Attachment

Think about a time when you've felt really down. How did you act (or react) toward your partner during your low mood? Did you withdraw or need to be alone? Or did you seek out your partner for help or want to be near her?

The way you relate to your partner when you're depressed has to do with your particular attachment style. Your attachment style—meaning your experience of receiving love and comfort from others—forms early on in life and is affected by the quality of the bond you had with your parents (Ainsworth et al. 1978). When you were upset or crying as an infant, your caregiver's ability to soothe you helped develop a secure bond. If your parents were unavailable or unable to soothe you—were angry toward you or distant—then your bond with them may have been negatively affected. Your experience of receiving love may not bring out feelings of warmth and joy for you, resulting in an insecure attachment style (Perry 2002). On the other hand, if your childhood experiences of love and bonding were strong and secure, the association with being loved brings feelings of caring, joy, and deep comfort. In this case, you're more likely to have developed a secure attachment style.

As an adult, the way you relate to your romantic partner is your adult attachment style (Hazan and Shaver, 1987). Psychologists have defined three basic styles of attachment, each stemming from your childhood attachment to your parent. The three primary attachment styles are *secure*, *anxious*, and *avoidant* (Bowlby 1988). As you read descriptions of each attachment pattern, you may notice what best describes your experience in relationships.

Secure Attachment

If you're securely attached, you feel comfortable being close to your partner. You generally have a positive view of yourself and others, and you don't fear being abandoned. Your relationships are based on trust and intimacy, and you tend to have strong relationships. When you're securely bonded to your partner, you see him as a secure base, as a source of support, even when you're depressed. You want to be close to her, she makes you feel better when you're down, and you feel sad when you don't get to be around her as much (Fraley and Shaver 2000). These are all healthy functions that reflect a strong bond.

In a secure relationship, you'll feel comfortable seeking comfort and support from your partner when you're upset or feeling down. In return, your partner is accepting and is able to soothe you and help you feel at ease. In secure relationships, both partners serve this role for one another when either partner is low (Johnson 2004). This means that when your partner is upset, he seeks you out as a safe haven and place of comfort (Bowlby 1988).

However, in insecure attachment, the balance in your relationship is off. It may feel like your partner is asking too much of you or overly seeking your time, attention, or affection. You may feel a lack of connection to your partner and be unable to be a secure base for them (Davila and Kashy 2009). This type of insecure attachment is called avoidant attachment.

Avoidant Attachment

If you have an avoidant attachment style, you tend to feel uncomfortable in close, intimate relationships. It probably feels like your partner wants more intimacy from you than you're willing or able to give. You are unlikely to share your thoughts or feelings with your partner. Your partner may complain that you are unable to be supportive of her in her times of need. She may feel that you're less emotionally invested in the relationship than she is. With avoidant attachment, you tend to have a cynical view of romance. You may have lower levels of commitment to your relationship, and you're at a higher risk for infidelity (DeWall et al. 2011). Being depressed tends to exacerbate all of these traits and may cause you to become even more detached from your partner.

With this attachment style, you tend to withdraw and retreat when there is distress or there are problems in your relationship; you're highly self-reliant. You tend to get overwhelmed by your partner's emotions and feel a need to escape. There's an expectation that others will not be there for you or be able to meet your needs, which may stem from your needs of safety and security not being met by one or both of your parents as you were growing up. Therefore, you feel safest when you're on your own. As a protective mechanism, you do not place a great deal of importance on emotions. Because of this, you're more likely to experience depression in the form of emotional numbing or avoidance. You tend to downplay upsetting events or minimize the significance of emotions such as despair, anxiety, or hurt, even when you're depressed.

Anxious Attachment

If you have an anxious attachment style, you tend to fear abandonment while you also have an urgent need for closeness. Your depression tends to be activated by feelings of rejection, loneliness, and fear, and it's difficult to tolerate those emotions. You may find that you're preoccupied with intimacy and worry a great deal about your relationship falling apart. Depression makes it difficult for you to handle feelings of possible rejection from your partner. You feel safest when you are close to him and feel highly uncomfortable when you're away from your partner—especially if there is any type of conflict or distress. However, this extreme need for closeness can damage your relationship because it can be difficult to ever fulfill. Your partner may end up feeling drained or overwhelmed. You tend to react strongly and quickly to any perceived problems in your relationship and are constantly on guard.

Depression can confuse and upset the process of secure attachment. It may seem difficult to soothe your own pain, let alone help someone else with hers. Depression puts a damper on your connection to your partner because you tend to withdraw from intimacy and connection during low periods rather than seek out your partner for comfort (Smith, Breiding, and Papp 2012). Perhaps you've been hurt before when you tried to reach out. Or maybe you assume your partner should know how to help, but she never seems to get it right. You may feel he expects too much of you, and rather than let him down, you shut down. You end up feeling frustrated and even more alone.

Evidence shows us that insecurely attached people have more trouble with their romantic relationships (Feeny and Noller 1990) and more trouble dealing with distress and conflict (Lopez and Gormley 2002). Psychologists at the University of Illinois found that the link between depression and marital dissatisfaction was very high for women who had an anxious attachment style but not for those who had secure attachment (Scott and Cordova 2002). In other words, having an anxious attachment style makes it more likely that you'll become depressed when you have problems in your marriage (Bifulco et al. 2002). Similarly, they found that those with an avoidant attachment style tended to report more depression and have more relationship problems (Holahan et al. 2005). Overall, insecure attachment is related to both depression and relationship distress.

Turning It Around

So what are you to do if your attachment style is insecure? Simply being conscious of your style of relating to your partner—and your partner's way of relating back—can positively influence your relationship. While you don't always have control over your attachment style, you can choose your behaviors. You can work to foster coping skills and behaviors that will help you ultimately feel more secure in your relationship.

Show Understanding

Couples who really hear each other are happier in their relationships and have lower levels of depression and anxiety (Fruzzetti and Iverson 2004). You can set the tone of caring and understanding in your relationship. Go out of your way to be receptive to the feelings your partner shares with you. Whether he's feeling burned out at work, distraught that he lost a job contract, or frustrated with a new home-improvement project, your partner will feel closer to you knowing that you understand how he's feeling. Show him you understand by listening without criticism or judgment and reflecting back what you hear him saying. It can be as simple as saying, "I can see you're upset about this" or "I'm sorry you're feeling discouraged." Allow him space to feel how he feels, and avoid rushing to fix things or make suggestions right away.

Get Comfortable with Conflict

Conflict is necessary for your relationship, but it gets a bad reputation. Many of us find conflict to be uncomfortable, even painful. There's a nagging feeling that if you're fighting with your spouse, something must be wrong. The truth is that conflict is inevitable and a normal part of two people sharing a life. And when handled adaptively, conflict can be beneficial. Conflict brings issues out into the open and helps clarify important topics. It is good to know what each member of your family is thinking and to be able to discuss these tough situations openly. When you're walking on eggshells, your intimacy suffers. In a partnership, addressing each person's point of view and clarifying your own perspective will help your relationship grow.

It's important to address small conflicts early on before they build and become overwhelming. Rather than let an issue simmer until it explodes, you should talk about the problem at an early stage. As you work through conflicts, you will create and maintain a more equitable, more fulfilling relationship. Both of you will feel secure when the balance of power between you is equal and you both feel comfortable expressing your opinions, knowing that you'll be heard and respected.

Discuss Your Future Dreams

Sharing with your partner your dreams for the future can make you feel closer and more secure in your relationship. A client named Rebecca said that one of her most intimate moments with her husband was when she shared her deepest dreams with him. Many years ago, she'd been very involved in writing short stories and fiction, even taking classes, sharing her work and getting tremendous feedback. But after getting married and having three kids, her writing had taken a backseat. One day at lunch, her husband Nathan asked her what her dreams were: what had she always wanted to do? She told him about her stories and writing courses and how she had once had a dream to pursue writing. As Rebecca told him how she felt, she discovered an even stronger desire inside of her emerging. Nathan was receptive about her writing and asked to read her work if she'd like. After this conversation, she began writing again and felt a renewed energy for a dream she thought she'd given up on. She felt bonded to Nathan for having shared and nurtured that dream with him.

Besides sharing your personal dreams with your partner, you may want to talk to your partner about some mutual dreams for your future together. Depression masks the future as dull and dreary, so it's nice to be able to dream about brighter times ahead. What do you want to be doing in five, ten, or twenty years down the line? How would life be different for both of you if your dreams were realized? What can the two of you do now to help make those dreams come true? When you build your aspirations together, you produce a sense of unity and security; you're in it together. You'll work together, and you'll reap the benefits together.

Be on Your Partner's Side

Loyalty is one way of showing that your relationship is a top priority. Find a way to let your partner know, on a daily basis, that you're in her corner. You might show your loyalty by standing up for your partner when she feels the world is against her. Let her know that you support what she's passionate about. Tell her that you're proud of how hard she works. Show her that you value what she values. When your partner feels confident that you're in her corner, it will add a sense of teamwork, security, and intimacy to your relationship.

Conclusion

While the uninvited guest, depression, doesn't come with a name tag, you can learn to identify it and address how it affects your love life. This chapter introduced the idea that, based on their attachment style, people who are depressed may respond to loved ones differently. Much of your attachment style in your current relationship likely developed over the course of your childhood and past relationships, but it continues to have an effect on your feelings of closeness and security in your current relationship. Learning to notice how you interact with your partner is the first step in making positive changes.

In the next chapter, you'll learn how to slow down your automatic reactions—some of which have been learned and become habit—and begin to exert more influence over how you respond to painful emotions. You'll find that making even small changes in your interactions can be tremendously helpful in your relationship.

chapter 3

Managing Painful Emotions

My clients, Alex and Heather were discussing their finances. Alex held a steady job with a regular salary. Heather's job was seasonal and inconsistent; there were no guarantees about how much income she could depend on. This was a particularly slow season, and the bills were starting to pile up.

The minute finances were brought up, Heather exploded in anger at Alex: "I don't know why I'm the only one managing these finances! I hardly am making any money, but you don't seem at all concerned, and you're certainly not making any changes to your spending habits! We'll be bankrupt next week, at this rate!" Alex tended to tune out when Heather started yelling like this, and he avoided talking about money. Meanwhile, she continued to grow more and more upset.

During our sessions together, we learned that the topic of strained finances brought up painful emotions of helplessness and failure for Heather. Unaware of how else to deal, she ended up driving a wedge between Alex and herself whenever these emotions came up. Rather than deal with two separate but pressing issues (one being the need to take a look at their finances and budget, the other being her feelings of helplessness and failure), she ended up pushing Alex further away from her. Wanting to avoid her strong emotions, Alex tended to shut down and retreat.

Managing painful emotions is one of the toughest parts of depression. Your feelings can be so overwhelming and unpleasant that it's difficult to know what to do with them. In trying to manage your emotions, you inadvertently end up pushing your partner away. It's likely you are not even aware of what you're doing, and it may feel confusing that your partner isn't responding in a more helpful manner.

Some of the actions that may cause problems include using your partner to manage your moods, taking out your anger on him, avoiding or denying your emotions, experiencing emotional overload, having judgments about your emotions, and withdrawing when you experience painful feelings. All of these behaviors are related to having difficult emotions and not knowing how to handle them in the context of your relationship.

This chapter is focused on helping you understand why negative emotions occur, when you are most likely to experience them, how they affect your coping style, and how to manage them. Rather than push your partner away when you feel anger, shame, sadness, pessimism, or other difficult emotions, you can learn to notice these patterns of negativity right away and to change your response. You can learn to deal with painful feelings and manage your moods, using such tools as emotional awareness, acceptance, attunement, self-soothing, and assertiveness. You can learn how to approach difficult emotions mindfully and bring this mindful awareness into your interactions with your partner.

Understanding Emotions

Have you ever wondered why we have emotions? Emotions evolved primarily to alert us to events in our lives that need attention. Bad feelings can sometimes serve as a warning signal that something is wrong or needs to be addressed. Anxiety often alerts us to danger; sadness allows us to slow down and evaluate meaning in our life; anger drives us toward action against a threat (McKay, Fanning, and Ona 2011). Other difficult emotions serve a purpose as well; shame helps us recalibrate our actions; grief allows us to appreciate loved ones and to connect with others who have lost someone.

Emotions can serve as a helpful guide for making sense of your experiences. For example, you might get a phone call from an old friend and feel happy after laughing with her. After hanging up the phone, you think to yourself, "I need to catch up with her more often." In this case, you've appraised the situation as positive, and you link your experience of talking to her with a feeling of happiness.

Intense emotions, on the other hand, are often a reaction to life-altering events that jar your sense of identity and order in the world. Major transitions in life are often associated with depression.

Major Transitions

It's fairly intuitive to know that when you are dealing with a major life event, such as the death of a family member, the loss of a job, or a serious physical illness, your risk of becoming depressed is greater. These are all losses, causing you to grieve the absence of someone or something that you had gotten used to having in your life. It often feels unfair. It often is unfair. Your sense of safety and security in the world is deeply shaken. Your sense of identity feels disjointed or confused. This loss of security and support, along with the realization that life is unpredictable, can cause you to feel hopeless and depressed.

If you have experienced a loss and didn't have a lot of support from others when dealing with it, have had multiple losses, or didn't have space to fully process a loss, your depression may be related to unprocessed grief. Another strong indicator of unprocessed grief is feeling a sense of avoidance or detachment about the loss.

Other transitions that can trigger depression include getting married, changing careers, becoming a parent, or moving to a new area. These events are usually associated with happiness, so it may be confusing when they bring about feelings of sadness or being overwhelmed. Whenever you go through life-altering changes, you can experience major stress as you adjust. Such life changes force you to reevaluate your role in the world, which can feel very unsettling.

My client, Maureen, for example, was thrilled when she got engaged to Mark. He was a loving partner and would be a great husband. As she began planning the wedding, however, she noticed that she would get waves of sadness. Told that this should be the happiest time of her life, she felt guilty and confused about what she was experiencing. The reality is that getting married brings up all kinds of thoughts and feelings about loss and love. She was losing her identity as a single person and was leaving her nuclear family to create a new family with Mark.

Marriage also made Maureen think about death and loss. When her grandfather had died, Maureen saw how her grandmother had been devastated to lose the love of her life. For Maureen, getting married to Mark meant that she would be building her life with him yet also might face losing him someday, which would break her heart. Maureen found herself feeling less close to Mark, avoiding intimacy, and shutting down, which effectively pushed Mark away. Maureen initially didn't know how to cope with the feelings of loss and sadness that were brought up by this major life transition of getting married. Once she recognized these emotions, whe was better able to respond to them.

Interpersonal Triggers

While major transitions can be triggers for depression, daily interactions can also bring out feelings of loss, rejection, jealousy, shame, or failure. Many people with depression are particularly sensitive to criticism from others and have difficulty managing these feelings. Even small amounts of constructive feedback may illicit strong feelings for you.

You may focus more on negative interactions because they naturally stand out to you. For instance, you may have a performance review with your boss in which she makes ten positive comments and gives you one area to focus on for improvement. If you are especially sensitive to criticism, you will focus on the negative comments, questioning where you went wrong, feeling ashamed and underappreciated. Criticism can feel like a personal attack on your character. Such powerful emotions might be hard to manage, leading you to feeling helpless and depressed.

If you're depressed, it's likely you have the most trouble dealing with the following painful emotions:

- Shame

- Regret

- Guilt

- Hurt

- Loss

While some of these painful emotions may stem from sources outside your relationship, they can easily seep into your interactions with your partner. Research confirms that negative emotions of anger and withdrawal, in particular, toward spouses are higher on days when job stress is high (Story and Repetti 2006). Having a stressful interaction with your boss or being saddled with someone else's project at work can easily overflow into your relationship at home.

Emotional Overload

Intense emotions are often a result of emotional overload. Perhaps you could have dealt with that extra project at work if that were all that was on your plate. Perhaps you could have dealt with your sister's mental illness, with frequent phone calls from her in desperate need of help from you, if that were the only stressor you faced. But add those stressors to the fact that you're caring for your aging father, trying to finish your taxes by April 15, and making an effort to work on your marriage. The emotional burden may become overwhelming, intense, and difficult to manage.

What happens to all those negative emotions that build up? Your moods, thoughts, and behaviors are highly interrelated. For instance, if you have a long commute home, and you're dreading it, thinking about how miserable you will be, you'll find yourself in a crabby mood even before you get in the car. So your thoughts (*I hate this commute*) about an activity (your commute) have affected your mood (producting irritability and anger).

Other times, your emotions become so strong that they drive your thoughts and behaviors. You might arrive home from your commute in an increasingly frustrated and irritable mood. This irritable mood makes it hard to connect with your spouse. Your thoughts about him (*He has no idea what I go through at work*) are affected by the mood you're in. And your behaviors are affected by your mood, perhaps telling your spouse that you're exhausted and don't feel like having dinner together because you just want to go to bed.

Harboring intense emotions without awareness and a healthy outlet is often the cause of depression. It depletes your energy, patience, and empathy. Whether the cause of your negative feelings is from an outside source (work, conflict with your daughter) or from a problem between your spouse and you, emotion-driven behavior takes a toll on your relationship.

Denying Your Emotions

Countless clients have talked about how bad it feels to feel ashamed, to cry, or to let others see their vulnerability. Our society gives us messages from a very young age that many emotions are unacceptable.

Certain emotions may have been discouraged in your home as you were growing up. For instance, one client discussed how she never disagreed or fought with her parents, because it was understood that asserting herself in this way would be met with a belittling or demeaning comment. Eventually, she learned that showing her emotions was simply unsafe. Others find that showing certain emotions, such as anxiety or worry, is easier than showing other emotions such as hurt, fear, or shame.

Distancing yourself from your emotions happens when you dismiss or try to push them away. Connecting to your emotions, on the other hand, is the process of allowing yourself to feel what you feel, when you feel it.

Connecting to Your Emotions

You might wonder, *Is it really worth it to connect to my emotions? I'd rather avoid feeling bad if I can.* As difficult as it can be, it is important to recognize painful as well as pleasant emotions and allow yourself to feel them. Once you start discovering and connecting with your full range of emotions, you will develop greater empathy for yourself and your partner, cope better with your emotions and your pain, and live a fuller life.

Developing Empathy

By being more attuned to your own emotions, you'll develop greater empathy for yourself and be better able to feel and show greater empathy for your partner. Research has shown that women who are depressed have more problems with "empathic accuracy"; they have difficulty accurately identifying their own thoughts and feelings, as well as identifying the emotions and thoughts of their partners (Gadassi, Mor, and Rafaeli 2011). The study also found that when women were depressed and their empathy was down, their mates also became less empathetic and attuned. Showing concern and empathy for your partner is a critical aspect of any healthy relationship, so fostering this ability, especially when you're depressed, is key.

Taking the Mask Off

It's important to recognize that ignoring or masking your emotions doesn't make them go away. In fact, ignoring your feelings usually makes them stronger, and this increasing intensity can lead you to find more extreme measures to try get rid of your emotions. You might find yourself drinking more to avoid feelings, or you might find yourself simply tuning out from life because you're numb to all emotions. When you numb your ability to be in touch with your painful emotions, you often numb out your connection to all of your emotions, including joy and humor.

Coping with Pain

Connecting with your emotions will help you cope with your pain. You can decrease the effect of painful emotions simply by being aware of your emotional state. You may worry that focusing on how you feel will make you feel worse, but research has shown the opposite to be true (Lieberman et al. 2011). For example, labeling your affect if you are scared, or stating "I'm terrified right now" while experiencing terror, will ultimately reduce the actual fear you feel (Kircanski, Lieberman, and Craske 2012).

Many people have trouble labeling their emotions because they worry that acknowledging negative feelings will somehow encourage them to feel negatively. "If I accept that I'm sad or depressed, isn't that like giving in?" one client asked. "Like I'm just resigning myself to being depressed?" While this concern is understandable, the answer is no. There is a difference between accepting and acknowledging how you feel in the moment and encouraging or reveling in that feeling.

Living a Full Life

Lastly, it is important to become attuned to your feelings because living a full life means embracing a broad range of emotions. To be human and to feel deeply means that you will have ups and downs. It would be impossible to have only happiness in your life. In fact, happiness would probably cease to feel like happiness if you had no other emotions to compare it to. Experiencing negative emotions serves to deepen your appreciation of positive experiences when they occur. Participating in the world fully means that you accept the range of feelings that naturally occur within you.

One way to think about your relationship to your emotions is to consider the concept of *emotional intelligence,* or how effectively you perceive and relate to your emotions. Couples where both partners show high levels of emotional intelligence express the most satisfaction in their relationships (Schröder-Abé and Schütz 2011). People who have high emotional intelligence are aware of their own emotions and are able to monitor and understand their own feelings. They also have the ability to manage their emotions, such as being able to calm down quickly or self-soothe when upset. Those high in emotional intelligence are sensitive to the feelings of others. Emotional intelligence is important to relationship quality; couples where both partners possess emotional intelligence are more committed and closer to one another (Schröder-Abé and Schütz 2011).

As with any area of life in which you want to increase your aptitude, you can work on improving your emotional intelligence. You can develop greater awareness of your emotions by learning and practicing some new skills. As you do, you will be not only learning to deal with your own painful emotions but also increasing your ability to be sensitive to your partner.

Developing Emotional Awareness

The process of noticing your internal reactions as they occur is called emotional awareness. It's about slowing down and being aware of your internal world. Approaching your emotions in this open, curious manner allows you greater flexibility as difficult emotions arise. To expand your emotional awareness and respond to your emotions in a compassionate way, you will need to acquire the tools of mindfulness, acceptance, and attunement.

Mindfulness

When something is troubling you in your relationship, it causes distress. It's common to respond to feeling upset by thinking about the *what-ifs* and *should-haves*. For example, you might think, *If I were a better partner, then we wouldn't be having these problems*, or *She should've known that would upset me.* In an attempt to relieve your pain, you may revisit the problem over and over again, playing out other scenarios or thinking about what you'll do in the future. There's the hope that if you could just figure out a solution, your mood will improve. Instead, a pattern of negative thinking sets in, where instead of solving the problem and moving forward, you get stuck in the past or become very attached to your pain. When you are focused on wishing things were different, your painful emotions are accentuated: *Where did I go wrong? Why do I always have so many problems?* You end up feeling more stuck, more discouraged with yourself and your partner, and you experience a downward spiral of negative emotions and negative thoughts (Segal, Teasdale, and Williams 2004).

Instead, mindfulness allows you to deal with your present, here-and-now experience. Rather than thinking about what could've or should've happened, you focus instead on your current reality. Mindfulness pulls you out of the past, bringing you into your present. The more attuned you are to your emotions, the better you'll feel.

Acceptance

A key aspect of mindfulness is having an accepting attitude toward your current emotions. Having acceptance doesn't mean accepting that you are going to be depressed for the rest of your life or that you love feeling down—quite the contrary. You can have acceptance while still working hard to make changes to help your mood and your relationship.

Acceptance has to do with acknowledging how you feel right now, in this very moment. It means accepting that right now, for whatever reason, you feel disappointed, or guilty, or sad. Acceptance is about being aware of where you're at emotionally; it doesn't mean that you love it or want it to be like this, but it does mean that you understand that there's no point in denying it or agonizing over it. Rather than wishing life weren't this way, you simply accept that right now, it is what it is.

Using mindfulness and acceptance skills, you can objectively observe your own actions, allowing you to walk yourself through difficult moods.

Exercise: Being a Nonjudgmental Observer

The next time you are upset, take the following steps to acknowledge the feelings in a nonjudgmental way.

1. **Label your emotions.** Start by allowing yourself to recognize the painful emotions that come up, and then name these feelings with descriptive terms. For instance, you might notice that you're feeling frustrated, sad, or hopeless. Then articulate how you feel and why you may feel that particular way right now.

    Example: *I'm feeling hopeless and empty in my relationship because my partner and I haven't had one meal together this week and we haven't had sex in five weeks.*

    Example: *I'm feeling ashamed because my spouse had a great day at work and I felt jealous as he discussed his success.*

2. **Rate their intensity.** Next, rate the intensity of your emotions on a scale of 1 to 10, with 10 being the most intense and 1 being the least intense. Rating the intensity of your emotional experience helps you look at your feelings dispassionately and helps you accurately label how you're feeling.

3. **Identify your willingness to feel the emotion.** Now identify your willingness to feel the emotion rather than push it away, ignore it, or criticize yourself for feeling this way. Give yourself permission to feel the way you feel. Rather than wasting energy wishing it weren't so, allow yourself to stay with the emotion.

4. **Avoid judgments.** You may notice yourself labeling your emotions as good or bad, desirable or undesirable. Instead, attempt to observe your emotions as if they were a separate entity from you. Remind yourself that the emotion is something you are experiencing. It does not define you.

Example: *It's understandable I would feel sad today, considering I am dealing with my friend's recent cancer diagnosis and given that I had a crummy day at work. It's neither good nor bad that I feel sad. It is what it is. I am experiencing some sadness right now.*

Practicing these steps whenever you feel bad will help you notice and accept your feelings and more easily work through them.

Attunement

When feelings are really strong, it often feels like they will never end. When you're feeling terribly sad or empty in the moment, it helps to recognize that negative emotions will come and go. This means being attuned to the bigger picture of how your emotions work.

Exercise: The Mood Pendulum

Think back to the last time you were really upset about something. How painful did the emotion feel at the time? Rate the intensity on a scale of 1 to 10, with 10 being the most painful, and 1 being the least painful.

Now, looking back, how long did you feel very upset? Did you feel less upset or more upset over time? Did the intensity of your feelings come and go?

What you will probably notice is that feelings are like waves crashing onto the sand: they ebb and flow. As surely as you're feeling negative emotions right now, you will likely feel other, more positive emotions soon.

Creating greater emotional awareness through mindfulness, acceptance, and attunement will put you in a better place to respond compassionately to painful feelings. Breaking free of rumination entirely, however, may also require taking a new approach to dealing with problems you encounter.

Breaking Free of Rumination

Emotions can get you stuck in trying to understand or answer why something happened: *Why did he leave me? Why can't I be different from how I am now? What went wrong in my life? Why am I always depressed? Why did I say that? Does she really love me?* You may retrace past mistakes, replaying scenarios over and over, searching. You've learned that staying mindful of your present moment is a strong antidote to this negative cycle of rumination; it puts you in touch with the here-and-now rather than the past.

Another way to approach rumination is to understand the deeper need that you're trying to meet.

Exercise: What's the Deeper Need?

The next time you catch yourself getting stuck in trying to understand why something happened, identify the core ruminative thought or feeling you're having. Do this as a nonjudgmental observer.

Next, think about what you're hoping to accomplish through your rumination. Ask yourself what would be different if you could understand or grasp the situation.

Example: *I'd understand why he said that.* Or *I'd understand why bad things always happen to me.* Or *I'd feel less hurt, and I could move on.*

Now, ask yourself, what emotional need are you trying to meet by understanding the situation?

Example: *To avoid feelings of uncertainty.* Or *to feel less ashamed.* Or *to feel happy and confident.*

Ask yourself if you can get your emotional needs met in other ways besides answering the question you're ruminating about. What are some concrete steps can you take?

Example: *I can boost my feelings of confidence by offering to help out a friend. I will call her right now.*

By taking such steps, you are letting yourself know that there is more than one way to meet your emotional needs, which will help you move on.

Maybe you'll never know the reason something did or did not happen. What you can have, however, is acceptance with the past. You can choose to say to yourself, *I don't know why this happened, and I may never fully understand it. But I do know that I've learned from it. And I know that I can choose to stop trying to understand it and choose instead to start living my life in the present.* The key is to make sense of the incident as best you can and to allow the rest to simply be a part of your past.

Taking this method a step further, you can use what you know about the past to serve as a guide for the future. When you ask what went wrong, are you trying to get back to feeling connected with your partner? If this is your deeper need, then you may be asking the wrong question. Instead, ask yourself, *What was working well when we were at our strongest?*

Exercise: What Works Well?

List the times when you and your partner have felt the most connected.

Example: *On our yearly vacation to Hawaii.*

Example: *When we first moved in together.*

Describe three unique aspects of those situations.

Example: *When we first moved in together, we both had less stressful jobs, we talked every morning over coffee before going to work, and we played tennis on Thursdays.*

Ask yourself how you could incorporate some of these positive things into your present life. Be as specific as possible. Clearly outlining the parameters will make it easier to commit to a goal. Ask yourself these questions:

1. Drawing from your past experience, what could you do now?

2. When could you make time for this?

3. Where would you do this?

4. How would you accomplish this?

Now put your plan into action.

An example of using the past constructively can be seen in the case of Simon and Kristi. They came to a session, beaming as they said, "We did it! Things have been so much better with us lately."

"We had our friends and family over for the weekend," Kristi continued. "Normally, I would've felt left out when Simon wanted to spend time with his friends. But I reminded myself to think about the past times we've hosted weekends, what's worked well and what hasn't. I was mindful of what I could contribute to the situation. Rather than getting stuck when I started to feel upset, I tried to be in the moment, to notice my experiences, and to be more proactive.

"There was a moment when I noticed myself feeling really nega-tively. Simon was playing cards with his friends, having a blast, and I felt ignored, left behind. But instead of withdrawing or leaving, or getting lost in my thoughts and being upset, I stopped to think about what I was really feeling at the moment. I realized I wanted to be part of what was going on. I saw that to feel included, I also had to do my part. So I accepted their invitation to join the game of cards for the second round, and I had fun! We got along well the entire weekend, and it feels like we're in a good place."

Kristi was able to catch herself before getting lost in rumination. She stopped to ask herself what she really was yearning for, and instead of searching for the answer to *Why do I feel left out?* she asked herself. *What can I do to help this feeling?*

Improving Your Coping Style

Some of the most intense negative emotions you experience may come from interactions with your partner. How you cope with these negative emotions when they arise can make a huge difference in how you feel.

Think about the last time your spouse hurt your feelings or let you down. Were voices raised? Was there a stormy silence? As with most couples, there's probably a pattern to how you handle negative emotions in your relationship. This pattern is called a coping style.

Coping styles are defense mechanisms; they're behaviors you use that make you feel safe when you feel hurt or attacked. The three primary coping styles are moving away from others, moving against others, and moving toward others (Teyber and McClure 2011). As with attachment styles, you usually learn these coping styles in childhood. If your family didn't give you a lot of support, for example, you probably learned to deal with problems on your own. If your family members were inconsistent or placed conditions on their love for you, you probably learned to seek out approval from others, but you also may have difficulty ever feeling truly accepted or secure.

While learning to rely on yourself or learning to please others may have worked to some extent as you were growing up, it's possible to overuse a coping style and become inflexible in how you relate to your partner. Being rigid in your coping style means that no matter what the situation, you respond the same way. Your ability to respond to challenging situations is diminished. One of the main reasons people tend to rely on a certain coping style is that they don't know how else to respond to the painful emotions they encounter. But no matter what your coping style, you can make changes for the better.

If You Move Toward Your Partner

If moving toward your partner is your coping tendency, you probably dislike conflict and feel uncomfortable if your partner is upset or dissatisfied. By pleasing your partner, you are seeking reassurance. If he feels better, then so do you. Pleasing your partner is effectively relieving your own anxiety. You're probably very caring and very good at taking care of others; you likely were the peacemaker growing up.

The downside can be that you end up blaming yourself for every conflict, regardless of the situation, meanwhile neglecting your own needs and increasing your chances for depression. You probably struggle with expressing and being on the receiving end of anger, overt displeasure, or hostility. If under relationship stress, you might focus on pleasing your partner and end up feeling overwhelmed or, alternatively, selfish if you ask for help. Again, this can lead to periods of depression and hidden resentment, where you've neglected your own needs and feelings for too long.

You can do something to change this. Remember that it's virtually impossible to please your partner all the time, and trying to do so may lead to feeling depressed. Remind yourself that your needs are a priority too. You're not doing your spouse any favors by sacrificing your own needs, because you may become resentful and depressed over time, causing more trouble down the line. Keeping your thoughts and feelings to yourself is also a way of pushing your partner away, because your partner never gets the chance to see the real you.

If you tend to move toward your partner, remind yourself that relationships are a two-way street, so you need to pay attention to what helps you feel nourished.

Consider Your Preferences

Rather than making decisions based solely on what your partner wants, practice expressing your own preferences.

- If cooking a meal together helps you feel closer to your partner, make a grocery list of what you'd like for dinner and let your partner know you'd like to make a date of it.

- If going to your office holiday mixer as a couple means a lot to you, let your partner know you'd like to go together.

- Practice expressing your feelings along with your preferences: "I'd like to attend the Saturday BBQ because it makes me feel good to connect with our neighbors."

- Look at your family schedule, and set aside personal time for yourself. Come up with a regular activity, like painting or yoga, and ask your partner to help you get the time for this.

Rather than assume your significant other knows what you need, let your partner know what will help you feel loved.

Watch for Signs of Emotional Dependency

Learn to separate your own feelings from your partner's feelings. Being overly concerned with your partner's mood can trigger depression, where your moods reflect whatever mood your partner is in. If there's emotional dependency, you may feel a little lost or empty without your partner there. Overidentifying with your partner's feelings is another form of avoiding your own emotions, so it's important to become attuned to this process.

If you notice that your mood often depends on your partner's mood, bring a sense of awareness to when these moments occur. In those moments, allow yourself space to experience your own emotions, rather than focusing on his. Remind yourself: *His feelings are not my feelings. We have separate experiences.* Giving yourself this separation will make room in the relationship for interdependence, which is a healthy mix of taking both of your wishes and desires into account. Your depression will be less likely to emerge when you're feeling more confident with your own feelings.

Lastly, be okay with saying no. While saying no may be uncomfortable at first, practice setting boundaries by gently but firmly saying no to taking on more tasks or overextending yourself. Remember, you're not rejecting your partner. You're just saying no to the request.

If You Move Against Your Partner

A tendency to move against your partner means you prefer to be in charge and in control of the situation. Your depression tends to come out in the form of irritability, hostility, and criticism. You're most likely to become defensive when your partner does something that causes you to feel ashamed or weak. You tend to go on the offensive, with a sense that it's better to attack before being attacked. It's likely that you're less trusting of your partner and are quick to blame her for things going wrong. Your partner may find your behavior intimidating or feel like she's "walking on eggshells" to avoid setting you off. The emotions that give you the most trouble are shame, sadness, and vulnerability. There's often a mindset that you must fight for yourself, and you often view your partner competitively.

You may become angry in response to feelings of defenselessness and impotence. You may believe that your partner won't listen unless you yell. You may worry that if you don't stand your ground, your partner will take advantage of you, knock you down, and trample all over you. Or maybe anger is the only way you know to express yourself. But intimidating your partner will end up only pushing her even further away. Other strategies can actually be far more effective in making you feel heard.

- Try asking questions first to see your partner's point of view before you share yours.

- Try taking a more vulnerable approach. Instead of showing anger, try expressing how you're feeling and why.

- Pay attention to your tone of voice. If your spouse hears your voice starting to rise, she may shut down or start raising her voice. If you adopt a gentler, more inviting tone, your spouse will listen more readily to you, and it will help you feel more calm in your discussion.

- Notice your body language. Keep your arms and hands relaxed and at your sides rather than crossed.

Take a time-out. When you notice emotion overload, you might say, "I'm feeling overwhelmed and need to take a break from talking about this. Can we come back to it in ten minutes?" Taking a time-out, or a break, is not the same as avoiding the discussion. However, it's essential that you come back to the discussion as promised, after taking a walk around the block or getting a drink of water. Having had space to clear your mind, you may find that both of you are better able to talk things through.

Softening your approach and showing more sensitivity will go a long way toward fostering effective communication.

If You Move Away from Your Partner

You tend to retreat and withdraw from your partner when tension occurs. You pride yourself on being self-sufficient and independent, yet sometimes your detachment involves a sense of numbing or avoiding how you really feel. It is very uncomfortable for you to feel that you need your partner. Any display of strong emotion is difficult for you to deal with, including sadness, anger, guilt, or grief, whether the emotional display is your partner's or your own. You feel overwhelmed by strong emotions and prefer to shut them out. When it comes to depression, you might find yourself avoiding talking about your problems or feeling emotionally detached from your partner. Using alcohol or drugs to shut off emotions is common for people with this tendency, and often comes with negative consequences.

Avoiding conflict can work well in some situations, but withdrawing and not letting your partner know how you feel when there is conflict can also end up making the situation worse. Your partner feels closed off from you or pushed away. Because of your avoidance of your emotions, you may also end up avoiding your partner's needs. But you can take some steps to help counteract your tendency to shut down.

Give Insight Into Your Actions

Your silence signals to your partner that something is wrong, and it ratchets up his anxiety. Rather than retreat without explanation, let your partner know what you're thinking. Make it clear that it's not a rejection of him but instead a reflection of your own emotional state. You might say, "I'm feeling myself shut down. I don't want to shut you out, but it's hard for me right now." When your partner knows what's going on inside, it's much easier for him to give you space and to feel more secure.

Plan Your Conversation

To help you address difficult situations, it may be helpful to choose a time and place to talk about specific issues that you'd just as soon avoid. A session of couples therapy accomplishes this purpose, but you also can set time aside at home. In this case, it's best to choose a quiet, comfortable location. You also may want to set a time limit for how long you'll spend discussing the topic, if doing this makes you more comfortable.

Remind yourself that investing time to talk about your relationship shows that you're committed to your partner. Seeing that you are making an effort to communicate may be very healing and reassuring for your partner.

Whatever your tendency—whether it's to move away, toward, or against your partner—it probably will take time and effort to change. This is because your communication style is something you've practiced naturally for a long time. But it is possible to strike a healthy balance, using a wider range of coping skills. It's best to be flexible in how you handle conflict with your partner so that you can respond to different situations appropriately. It's also important to recognize your habitual way of relating to your partner so that you can consciously decide how to respond.

Communicating Assertively

So often, the way we communicate with one another feels ineffective, frustrating, or overwhelming. You may find that you hesitate to talk about important topics for fear of criticizing your partner or for fear of being criticized. Alternatively, you may become angry when your spouse fails to get it. Especially for those with depression, it's very common to expect others to already know how you feel or expect them to understand intuitively what has gone wrong. Clear communication with your partner can lead to better results in meeting both of your needs. When you're communicating more effectively, you'll notice that your feelings of depression will lift.

You may have noticed that you get different results based on how you communicate with your partner. For instance, imagine that your husband told you last week that he would pick out the dates for your kids' summer camp. The end of the week rolls around, and he hasn't done it. You wait another week, but still no camp dates. You're upset and frustrated that your husband didn't follow through. So what do you do?

1. Sign the kids up for camp, post the schedule on the bulletin board, and say nothing.

2. Over dinner that evening, when your husband asks what's wrong, explode and say, "I'm surprised you even noticed I'm upset! You never pay attention to anything! This house would fall apart if it weren't for me!"

3. Say something like this: "Honey, let's sit down and figure out the summer schedule. It's bothering me that it's still up in the air."

These three possible responses typify the most common communication styles: (1) passive communication, (2) aggressive communication, and (3) assertive communication.

Clearly, aggressive communication (exploding at your partner) is a hurdle to effective communication. If you are communicating aggressively, you are pushing away your partner by demeaning him and valuing your own perspective above his.

On the other hand, passive communication can be equally damaging, if not more so. Passive communication means you're not talking directly about the issue or issues that come up. It's a stalemate, and the silence tends to breed resentment in both of you. Avoiding problems doesn't make them go away; it usually makes them worse, because there's no chance for resolution. Your partner may not really know how you feel, and you may feel resentful that nothing is changing. You may be avoiding conflict in the moment—there is no arguing, no yelling, no tears—but you also are losing the ability to connect with your partner on a genuine level.

Assertive communication strikes a balance, using honest communication that fosters a dialogue between the two of you. Assertive communication is a balanced way of expressing your needs and concerns while being respectful of your partner.

You can work on communicating assertively. The key lies in your willingness to say the things that you are feeling in a manner in which your partner can hear you. When you approach your relationship with openness and a willingness to hear your partner's perspective, while also expressing your own point of view, you're fostering true intimacy.

How to Be Assertive If Your Style Is Passive

If you tend to be a passive communicator, there's a good chance that employing the strategy of acting as if you were more assertive will help you become comfortable with being more assertive. The idea here is that feeling follows action. Even though you're less than confident on the inside, you can act as if you felt confident. When you start behaving more assertively, feelings of confidence and self-assuredness will follow.

My client Fiona was working on being more assertive in her relationship with her husband Seth. She was naturally shy, and Seth usually had pretty strong opinions on most topics. Her tendency was to be passive and to go along with Seth's perspective. She talked with Seth about her tendency to hold back, and he expressed to her that he really valued her opinion and actually wished she were more willing to speak her mind.

Fiona practiced being assertive by first noticing her initially passive response and then turning it into a more honest, assertive one by acting as if this were her natural communication style. For example, Seth wanted to buy a new car, so he asked Fiona what she thought about the idea. Her first reaction was a passive one: "If you think it's a good idea, sure, whatever you want." She realized, however, that this response didn't actually convey what she really felt about the situation. Instead, she considered her true feelings and then said in a confident voice, "I've thought for a while now that it might be time to buy a new car, since we've had so many problems with the old one breaking down. I think it would be a good investment. Let's talk about which cars we might consider that would best fit our family and our lifestyle."

Exercise: Acting as If

Take these measures to be more assertive:

- Notice when you're most likely to retreat from conversations. Is there a particular theme? A topic, like religion or politics? Does it have to do with decision-making or with conflict or tension in a discussion? As you take note of the kinds of conflict you avoid, think about what you would like to handle differently.

- Rehearse using *I-messages* that convey assertiveness. Begin your statements with "I think…" or "My perspective is…" or "I need…."

- Focus on making eye contact, standing up straight with your head held high, while also relaxing your body and keeping an open stance. Confident posture aids assertiveness.

- Develop your perspective privately before you share your thoughts with your partner. You may want to write in your journal or read up on the issue.

- Let your partner know that you're actively working on being more assertive. This sets the stage for both of you to be prepared for some changes in your relationship dynamic. Let your partner know that the reason you're working on this is to help your depression and to have a stronger relationship with each other.

- Encourage your partner to ask you questions and seek your input on decisions that you make as a couple. You could say, "I'd like to be more involved in budgeting our finances." Or "Let's sit down together and take a look at our options for buying a home."

- Offer to help when your partner has a problem. It may feel uncomfortable at first, but you probably have a lot of insight and knowledge to share. Offer help in a gentle but direct fashion. For example, you could say, "I've had that experience before. Here's what helped in my case."

The more you interact in an assertive manner, the more self-assured you'll feel. This is how feelings follow action. Doesn't it feel empowering?

How to Be Assertive If Your Style Is Aggressive

If your style of communication tends to be aggressive, you can work on being assertive without aggression. When you sense you are about to react aggressively, you can stop and modify your response.

Take the story of my client Daniel and his wife Collette. Daniel tended to respond aggressively to Collette. Both partners had feisty personalities, but Daniel found himself reacting strongly to neutral situations. His tendency to be aggressive was starting to bother him. He told me, "I don't want to be angry all the time. My kids notice it, and I worry how it affects them. Being angry doesn't feel good, but it's almost an automatic reaction." To start changing his communication pattern, Daniel worked to notice and modify his tone of voice and the type of words he used when expressing his opinion.

When Collette brought up the topic of having friends over for dinner, he practiced being assertive. His initial response was to yell, "Are you kidding me? We already have a million commitments, and I'm working overtime. No way we're having a bunch of people over for dinner!" But he stopped himself, recognizing that this response was more likely to cause a fight than to address the problem. Instead, he responded calmly, "I like having friends over and entertaining, and I know you do too. My first reaction, though, is that I'm feeling overwhelmed by work. It might make sense to plan for a party next month when things are better for both our schedules."

Notice how Daniel first acknowledged that the idea of entertaining friends, in and of itself, was a pleasant one. Then he disclosed his internal reaction to the suggestion. Finally, he spelled out a possible solution. By being aware of his natural reaction to yell and slowing down instead, Daniel was able to more effectively say what he was thinking without becoming more angry and upset. Aggressive communication disrupts intimacy and places strain on your relationship. By speaking to your partner assertively and calmly, you are keeping your intimacy intact.

Choose Your Battles

If you tend to have an aggressive communication style, another way to help your relationship is to address the issues that you are most passionate about and let go of the ones that matter less. That is, choose your battles wisely.

When an issue arises, check in with yourself before simply reacting. Consider what you'll gain or lose from confronting this particular issue. Look at how outcomes may differ based on how you approach the topic. Then choose to let it go or respond appropriately.

Exercise: Choosing Your Response

Whenever you feel your emotions rise, stop and imagine what a really calm, dispassionate person might say or do in this situation. Now act as if you were that person, imitating what that person might do:

- Let the other person have the last word.

- Back off a subject and let it go.

- Try to look at the situation from the other person's point of view.

- Communicate clearly and respectfully.

Ask yourself how you might communicate your passion without using harsh or destructive words. Try using I-messages, such as, "I feel strongly about this issue because it's affected my life in these ways."

If all of this feels unnatural at first, remind yourself that you are acting from choice-driven behavior instead of emotion-driven behavior.

Use Humor

You can use humor to defuse tense situations, but never use humor at the expense of the other person. Humor is helpful when it diffuses tension, but it can make situations worse if it's sarcastic or mean-spirited. If you're not sure about how your humor comes across to your partner, ask. Using humor can bring people together, help you take yourself less seriously, and ease a tense situation.

Conclusion

When you're actively aware of how you cope with negative emotions, you have more control over how you choose to interact with the world around you. It's the small, day-to-day interactions that make or break your relationship, and being aware of your inner state might make the difference between snapping at your partner or instead saying, "I'm in a bad mood right now. I don't want to take it out on you. If I seem upset, know that it's not anything you did."

It takes care and consideration to be aware of how your moods might be affecting your partner. After all, moods can be contagious. Have you ever noticed that when you're talking with someone who's excited and enthusiastic, you're more likely to leave the conversation feeling optimistic? Similarly, have you found that speaking with someone who is really upset can cause you to feel hopeless as well? Any time you interact with your spouse, you're bringing your energy into the dynamic. It's important to consider what type of energy it is that you're bringing.

Increasing your emotional awareness, adapting your coping style, and communicating assertively are assets you can bring to your relationship, starting today. By acknowledging and accepting your own feelings, your relationship will have room for flexibility and growth. When you let go of struggling with your pain, you will have more energy to devote to your inner well-being and the well-being of your relationship.

chapter 4

How to Connect with Your Partner When You're Worried

When you think about being depressed, you may not immediately think about the concept of anxiety or think that depression and anxiety are related at all. My experience in working with countless people has been that anxiety and worry are, in reality, a huge part of the struggle with depression. Moreover, I've found that anxiety and worry cause a great deal of conflict in relationships.

The research supports these notions. Depression and anxiety are so frequently seen together that many researchers believe you are more likely to experience both than to experience only depression (Rapaport 2001). And couples where one partner has anxiety are likely to have higher relationship stress and lower satisfaction than couples where neither partner is anxious (McLeod 1994).

What does mixed depression and anxiety look like? With mixed depression and anxiety, you'll notice certain symptoms:

- Difficulty concentrating
- Trouble sleeping

- Low energy

- High irritability and worry

- Hypervigilance, or a feeling of being constantly on guard

- Expectations of the worst

- Hopelessness about the future

- Feelings of worthlessness (Rivas-Vazquez et al. 2004)

A combination of anxiety and depression may affect your relationship in quite a few ways. This chapter explores how you may be anxiously attached and what may trigger your worries and offers some techniques to reduce your anxiety and break the anxiety pattern in your relationship. You will learn how to use the skills of tuning into your partner, gratitude, and loving-kindness to help you connect to your partner even when you're worried.

Anxious Attachment

Chapter 2 discussed the three attachment styles: secure, anxious, and avoidant. If you have an anxious attachment style, you're more likely to develop anxiety and depression and are more likely to have relationship problems (Jinyao et al. 2012). These problems often center around lacking trust or feeling insecure in the relationship, noticing faults in the other person, and feeling overwhelmed by relationship issues.

What does attachment anxiety look like in a relationship? Well, everyone tends to act anxiously attached in the early stages before you're officially together (Eastwick and Finkel 2008). When you first fall in love, you feel consumed by the need to be close to your new love; you're constantly thinking of the other person, and you're desperate to be around him. This need serves the purpose of pulling you closer to your partner and helping to secure your bond. But if you have an anxious attachment style, the constant need for connection and the constant preoccupation with your partner continue throughout your relationship. And they start to harm your bond because it's hard to satiate your need for closeness. For example, even after seven months with her partner, my client Tabitha felt uncomfortable whenever she went for more than a day without seeing Steve. If she couldn't reach him by phone or text, she would start worrying that he was losing interest in their relationship or was going to break up with her. When Tabitha would reach Steve, it never felt like enough. She always wished that their conversations would last longer or that he would express more affection for her. Even though Steve was affectionate and attentive, Tabitha paid greater attention to the few instances when he was less affectionate. She would point these moments out to Steve, asking what was wrong or if he still cared for her.

People who have attachment anxiety tend to see their partners as inattentive and reluctant to commit (Kunce and Shaver 1994), interpret their partner's behavior as negative (Collins 1996), overestimate the degree of relationship conflict, and overestimate the negative effects of their conflicts (Campbell et al. 2005). In other words, if you are anxiously attached, it's likely that you feel your relationship is in dire peril more often than it really is. Things may feel worse to you than they really are, and you may be underestimating how stable your relationship is.

When you start to notice that worry and anxiety about your relationship are taking hold, you can remind yourself that you have a tendency to overestimate what's bad. Rather than believe your worries are a certain sign of trouble, you can challenge yourself to look at the aspects of your relationship that are strong. You can recognize that while your worries may feel very real, there is a great deal of evidence showing that your relationship is strong, stable, and loving. For Tabitha, this might mean saying to herself, *When I don't hear from Steve, I jump to the conclusion that he's lost interest. But just yesterday he wrote me a sweet note, and I know he has no intention of leaving. Just because Steve's not here, it doesn't change our feelings for each other. And I know this feeling of worry will pass soon.*

Worrisome thoughts can be a trigger for relationship anxiety. The next exercise allows you to rate your level of attachment anxiety and will help you recognize the kind of thoughts that tend to trigger your anxiety. The list of common relationship worries in the exercise is adapted from Eastwick and Finkel (2008):

Exercise: Rating Your Attachment Anxiety

To gauge your level of attachment anxiety, rate how closely you agree with each statement on a scale of 1 to 7, where a rating of 1 means that you strongly disagree, 2 means that you disagree, 3 means that you disagree somewhat, 4 means that you neither disagree nor agree, 5 means that you agree somewhat, 6 means that you agree, and 7 means that you strongly agree.

- *I need a lot of reassurance that my partner cares about me.*

- *I worry about being abandoned by my partner.*

- *I wish that my partner's feelings for me were as strong as mine for him/her.*

- *I worry that my desire to be very close will scare my partner away.*

- *If I can't get my partner to show interest in me, I get upset or angry.*

- *When I'm not close to my partner, I feel somewhat anxious and insecure.*

- *I resent it when my partner spends time away from me.*

- *Sometimes I feel I force my partner to show more feeling/commitment.*

- *I get frustrated if my partner is unavailable when I need him/her.*

- *I often want to merge completely with my partner, and I worry that this could scare him/her away.*

- *I worry a fair amount about losing my partner.*

- *I worry that I might not have a future with my partner.*

- *When my partner disapproves of me, I feel really bad about myself.*

Now add up the numbers to get an attachment-anxiety score. If your score is 78 or higher and you experience such worries often and at this level of intensity, then you have a high level of attachment anxiety.

You may fluctuate within the spectrum of anxiety, meaning that sometimes you strongly relate to these sentiments while at other times you don't. You may notice these sentiments intensify during particularly stressful times or periods of depression. And while it's normal and even healthy to want your partner to be around often and to value your partner's opinion, attachment anxiety tends to be harmful for relationships.

The problems begin when your anxiety about your relationship is so pervasive that it interferes with trust and intimacy. This desperate sense of connection can end up producing the very thing you most fear. Such worries, if left unchecked, can be so strong and powerful that they may seem insatiable to your partner and end up alienating you from one another.

In the last exercise, you probably identified with some worry thoughts more than others. Being attuned to what you worry about and to what may trigger your worry is an important step toward breaking your anxiety pattern.

Understanding Your Worry Triggers

What causes these worried, anxious thoughts about your relationship? Anxious thoughts are commonly reinforced by a pattern of worry triggers, and the initial trigger is usually a sensation of danger or threat to your relationship.

Relationship Fears

A sensation of danger begins when you detect a threat to your relationship, such as when having an argument with your partner (Saavedra, Chapman, and Rogge 2010). Anything that causes you to feel that your relationship is in jeopardy is like a bright red flag, and it can feel like your future together is at stake. For instance, if you have a disagreement with your spouse, you may start imagining that your partner will leave you. Research has shown that when your mind encounters a situation like this that feels threatening—even if it's an imagined threat—you feel as bad as if you were experiencing the actual event (Hayes et al. 2004).

As you imagine what could go wrong, this worry activates your internal response network. This response network, sometimes referred to as fight-or-flight, triggers physical changes in your body to help prepare you for danger. So when you start to get stressed out or worried, your body will react as if it actually needed to do something to help you avoid the feared object or event. Your sympathetic nervous system kicks into gear, causing you to have tunnel vision, racing thoughts, tension in your body, and a general feeling of restlessness or of being keyed up.

Anxiety Sensitivity

As if worrying this way weren't enough, the physical sensations that accompany anxiety can trigger further worry. People who have *anxiety sensitivity*, a condition identified by Reiss and McNally (1985), are much more attuned to their own bodily sensations, like rapid heartbeat, and they tend to have heightened arousal to stress. If you have anxiety sensitivity, which is common in those with depression and anxiety, you're more likely to feel scared or threatened by your own negative emotions (Sauer-Zavala et al. 2012). The feeling of being overwhelmed by strong emotions, such as anger, fear, or sadness, may cause you to have even more difficulty with your relationship, since being a part of a couple can activate so many strong feelings.

Worrying and Rumination

The overwhelmed, fight-or-flight, physical response that goes along with worry can often be very upsetting. You may feel like you're going crazy or losing control. At the same time, you're trying to make sense of why your body is so anxious. All of the energy and discomfort you experience when you're worried causes you to want to do something about it, to relieve the feeling.

The process of worried ruminating—trying to find a solution to your anxiety—often makes you feel like you're being proactive about a problem. You may weigh all your options, going through every scenario and every potential outcome, vividly picturing what may happen. This level of worry often becomes counterproductive, however, as you end up feeling more stressed out, more uncertain, and more out of control, because there's no identifiable action that will solve anything. A helpful alternative is to focus less on *doing* something with your emotions and instead focus on *being*. This means allowing your emotions to simply exist and have a space to be as they are. Ironically, when you allow yourself this space, you actually create more room for feeling at peace and feeling at ease.

Managing Worry with Mindfulness

A critical step in helping to ease worry is to identify and sit with your underlying emotions. In other words, when you have those worrisome thoughts, it's important to ask yourself what other emotions you're experiencing. And it's vital that you not judge or criticize yourself for feeling the way you do. Instead, you can learn to notice in a mindful and compassionate way what emotions or feelings are associated with your worry.

You may discover fear of abandonment, fear of rejection, fear of judgment, feelings of unworthiness, and feelings of resentment, all of which are commonly associated with anxious attachment. While you may not think these emotions are necessarily desirable, it's important to pay attention to them if you have them. Remember that tolerating your emotions is the goal here; this means that rather than jump to do something about your worried and upsetting thoughts, you need to take a step back and sit with the underlying emotions.

When you act on impulses that come from painful emotions, it actually makes the emotions feel more intense (Linehan 1993).

Worry will often trick you into thinking that you have to respond a certain way. Worry is urgent, insistent, and persistent. But you can form a new relationship with worried thoughts and feelings. When you notice worried thoughts creeping in, it's really helpful to allow yourself space to consciously decide how you wish to react. The process of mindfulness allows you to do this.

Using Mindfulness Practices

You'll recall the idea behind practicing mindfulness is that by directing and focusing your attention inward, observing your thoughts and bodily sensations as they come and go, you're able to begin to experience your thoughts and feelings here in this very moment. Instead of getting lost thinking about the past or worrying about the future, you notice your immediate experiences.

The most important idea is to bring a sense of nonjudgmental acceptance to your mindfulness exercises. This means that whatever you notice is allowed to just be; there's no right or wrong way to feel. Being mindful is about trying to really notice what is there and letting it sit.

Mindful breathing is one way to practice mindfulness. Diaphragmatic, or deep, breathing activates your parasympathetic nervous system, helping your body to slow down to a state of calm. This practice is most effective if you do it on a daily basis (even five minutes a day is helpful), but you can also use it to help manage your anxiety in moments when you notice worry starting to creep up. Slow the process down and allow yourself to have at least ten to fifteen minutes of reflection.

Exercise: Diaphragmatic Breathing

To begin, find a comfortable, quiet spot where you can either sit comfortably or lie down without being disturbed.

1. Begin by focusing on your breath. Notice the natural flow of your breathing, in and out.

2. Next, inhale through your nose for three long counts. As you inhale, imagine the breath flowing down through your lungs into your abdomen. Allow your abdomen to expand as you breathe in. Place your hand on your stomach and feel your stomach filling up like a balloon filling with helium.

3. Gently hold the breath for another three counts.

4. Finally, exhale through your mouth for three extended seconds. As you exhale, retract your stomach as you push out the air.

As you focus on deep breathing, it can be helpful to repeat a mantra to help you feel centered. It might be as simple as thinking the words *calm* as you inhale and *release* as you exhale. You can imagine that the energy you're breathing in is calming and nourishing, and then, as you exhale, feel the tension and worry slip away.

The next exercise can be done along with your breathing exercise. It adds the dimension of tuning in to how your body feels in the moment. Body awareness adds to your sense of balance and holistic awareness of yourself, because it shifts your focus away from worried thoughts and onto what your body is doing.

Exercise: Body Awareness

In a comfortable seated position or lying down, gently close your eyes.

1. Take a few moments to find your rhythm of breathing, inhaling and exhaling slowly. As you practice deep breathing, gently turn your attention to how your body responds to your breath.

2. Pay attention to the sensations in your body, giving attention to each part; starting at your feet, moving up your legs, through your torso and up to your neck, shoulders, arms, and head.

3. As you bring awareness to each area of your body, notice any sensations such as tingling, tension, warmth, or cool temperature.

4. When you notice a sensation, label it. Labeling means that when you have a physical sensation, such as tightness in your chest or a knot in your stomach, you take a moment to say to yourself, *I'm noticing that I am feeling the sensation of* _____ .

5. Be aware of any urges to move or to change positions. While it's okay to shift, also experiment with the feeling of sitting still, resisting the urge to scratch an itch or to move to a more comfortable position. How does it feel to sit with the tension?

As you take the time to quietly be with your body, you may notice a heightened sense of being connected to your physical self.

Noticing Your Thoughts

Before I discovered mindfulness, I thought that my thoughts were absolute truths. If I thought something was wrong, it was wrong. If I thought something was scary, it was scary. The relationship was one of unquestioning acceptance. But mindfulness teaches you that thoughts and the way things are don't always have a 1:1 correlation. There's not just one, ultimate version of reality. Instead, your thoughts are like a commentator, reporting on the happenings in your world from your point of view, which may be extremely biased.

Rather than view your thoughts, such as *I cannot stand being away from my partner* or *I cannot tolerate this anxiety*, as absolute truths, mindfulness helps you to distance yourself and let go of such black-and-white statements. As you move away from seeing your thoughts as a tool to judge and predict, you can learn instead to use thoughts as a way to observe and note happenings. You will find yourself noting, *I notice myself saying I cannot tolerate this pain. While I prefer not to feel this way, I'm able to tolerate it now in this moment.* You will be able to reframe and disengage from painful thoughts when they are hurting you.

Exercise: The Commentator

The next time you begin to worry, take a few minutes to move away from being so actively involved in the conversation in your head. Observe your inner dialogue as if it were that of a character in a script that you were reading. Try to answer these questions.

- What does the character think and say?

- What previous experiences inform the way the script is written or how the character interprets things?

- As an outside observer, what insight do you have about what the character is going through?

Next, imagine that you're listening to the radio and your thoughts are those of a radio commentator. What does the commentator say? What tone of voice is the commentator using? Might the commentator's observations be different from yours, depending on his or her mood or preconceived notions?

When you are able to get some distance and witness your thoughts as an outsider, your thoughts and emotions have less power over you.

This next mindfulness practice allows you to notice your thoughts as if you were observing leaves floating on a stream. This exercise can be done with a period of deep breathing and can work well when you find yourself worrying. Allow five minutes for this exercise.

Exercise: Leaves on a Stream

Gently close your eyes and turn your attention to your stream of consciousness, the voice inside you that states your thoughts.

You may notice that you have a variety of thoughts as you sit with them: *Why am I doing this? How long have I been sitting here? I wonder if it's working.* Take the approach of recognizing each thought, acknowledging it, and then gently letting it go.

To help the process of letting your thoughts go, imagine a flowing stream in your mind. Picture this stream, perhaps in a wooded area, as it gently moves through the rocks and swooshes by. As each thought comes to mind, imagine that you can take that thought and place it onto a leaf. Now place the leaf on the water and watch the leaf float away. Another thought will probably pop up. Take that thought and place it onto another leaf, allowing it to be swept up by the stream.

Watch the stream flow by and notice how you get a sense of distance from your thoughts. Rather than your thoughts being who you are, you can start to see them as experiences that will come and go.

Noticing Your Emotions

You also can get some distance from your emotional reactions by labeling them. Noticing and labeling your emotions decreases their power, as it reinforces that you are not your feelings. That is, your feelings come and go, but you are a constant.

Studies have shown that labeling your emotions reduces negative emotional arousal, especially with anxiety (Lieberman et al. 2011). Labeling helps you to accept painful emotions as part of your repertoire of emotions and also helps you see that your feelings don't have to drive your behavior. Instead of fearing your emotions as if they were an unwanted visitor invading your body, you can begin to see them less with fear and more with curiosity and understanding.

Exercise: Labeling and Reframing Your Emotions

When you have an upsetting thought, emotion, or urge, take the following steps.

1. First label the emotion by saying to yourself, *Now I'm having the feeling of* _____ . Fill in the blank with the emotion you're having, such as sadness, anger, worry, or whatever best describes the emotion.

2. When you feel a distressing urge to do something, say to yourself, *Now I notice that I have the desire to* _____ . Fill in the blank with whatever urge you're having.

3. Remind yourself that having an urge does not equal acting on that urge.

4. Now reframe they way you can handle the emotion. State your emotion and what—if anything—you're going to do with that emotion. For example, you could say to yourself, *I have the urge to make a nasty comment. However, I am choosing to refrain from uttering the comment out loud.*

As you do this exercise, you're separating out your urges from your actions, allowing room for conscious decision-making.

When you notice yourself starting to become overwhelmed by worry, take a moment to ask yourself what other emotions might be coming up in relation to the situation. Anxiety often serves as a secondary emotion, meaning it's a reaction to something else that's more fundamental. For example, my client Jane found that she became anxious before and after PTA meetings at her daughter's school. After exploring her emotions, she found that she had some feelings of anger for the way some of the other moms were treating her. Her anxiety was actually a secondary emotion, whereas the primary (and, to her, less acceptable) emotion of anger was more central to how she really felt. Anxiety was the offshoot of her unlabeled and unexpressed anger.

The following exercise should help you identify which emotions you feel more comfortable with and which ones cause you to have anxiety.

Exercise: Expanding Your Emotional Comfort Zone

Take a moment to look at the list below:

Shame, fear, happiness, joy, doubt, anger, sadness, delight, passion, self-consciousness, sympathy, desire, embarrassment, amusement, emptiness, abandonment, danger, worry, pride, pain, indignation, loved, empathy, anticipation, surprise, disgust, envy, pity, courage, patience, relaxation, hopeful, confusion, wonder, contentment, vengeful, compassionate, nervous, neglected, brave, restless, rejected, resentful, pleased, confident, guilty, annoyed, safe

Which of these can you identify with? Which emotions represented in the list do you feel most at ease with? Which emotions are you less comfortable experiencing or do you feel the least frequently?

The next time you notice worry or anxiety start to bubble up, ask yourself, *What other emotions might I be feeling about this situation?*

Again, anxiety sometimes serves to distract you from recognizing—and dealing with—other painful emotions or emotions that you have more difficulty accepting. By listening to the anxiety and by looking for what it's trying to tell you, you will find it easier to effectively address the real issues.

For Jane, doing this exercise meant acknowledging her anger. Even though having feelings of anger about her PTA experience was uncomfortable, because she saw herself as a kind person who got along well with others, she realized that it was okay to acknowledge the reasons she experienced these feelings. Allowing herself to experience her anger, in small doses, helped her habituate to these feelings. The experience of anger became less frightening. Instead, she saw it as a signal that she needed to make some changes in the kind of people she let into her life.

Of course, anger is not the only difficult emotion that people experience. For example, my client Peter almost always felt tense and restless. He worked long hours and didn't experience much pleasure during downtime. After examining his feelings, he realized that he stayed so busy because spending time with himself, with nothing to do, made him edgy and uncomfortable. To deal with his anxiety, Peter realized that he needed to develop a new relationship with the experience of quiet relaxation and self-reflection.

As you practice mindfulness, you may notice that you have strong judgments about certain emotions. Lucas, for instance, realized that it okay to feel depressed and cynical, but he hated the experience of anxiety: "I shouldn't feel this way. It's weak to have anxiety." His primary feeling of anxiety would snowball into secondary feelings of self-loathing and shame. Instead of punishing yourself for your natural feelings (because you can't really choose how you feel), remind yourself that it's okay to feel whatever emotion it is that comes up in the moment. You might remind yourself that *Feeling anxious is part of life. I don't love it, but it doesn't make me a bad or defective person to have anxiety.*

With depression, many people have trouble handling positive feelings. Laura, a graduate student in psychology, had trouble knowing how to react to being happy. She told me how a series of illnesses and losses in her family during adolescence had shaped her sense that life was one series of painful events after another. So when things started to go well—she was enjoying her graduate courses, her friends, and her new girlfriend—she began to worry that something would come along to crush her happiness. Her primary feeling of happiness caused secondary emotions of anxiety and fear.

Laura worked on accepting her feelings of happiness. She reminded herself, *It's okay to feel happy and enjoy the fact that life is good right now.* She learned that even though happiness might not last forever, enjoying the people she loved and finding pleasure in her graduate work didn't mean that she was tempting fate. She learned to trust her positive emotions. While it took some getting used to, she found that letting happiness into her life was the biggest step she could take in easing the depression that had been a part of her life for so long.

Anxiety in Relationships

In relationships where one partner is more worried than the other, there is a common pattern that couples tend to fall into. It goes something like this.

You feel apprehensive about something and can't stop thinking about it. When, in an attempt to be proactive, you communicate your worries to your partner or try to solve the problem with him, you may not get the response you're looking for. Instead, you end up feeling ignored or marginalized. Meanwhile, your partner may feel like nothing he does or says is ever good enough. This can end up making him feel insecure about your relationship or your feelings for him. He feels helpless to soothe you or unable to enjoy time with you. The situation is exhausting for both of you. While you continue to feel worried and anxious, your partner feels drained by conversations that seem to go around in circles.

It may be difficult for your partner to understand why you're so worried. Your partner may have said something like "It's not a big deal, so don't worry about it." Or "Just don't think about it!" But it's not as easy as that, is it? You wish you didn't worry this way, but you can't seem to stop. Once worry takes hold, it's hard to let it go. The more you try to escape the thought, the more it consumes you.

Anxiety can be a deeply rooted element in your life that predates the experience of anxiety in your relationship. For example, a client of mine, Kate, doesn't remember a time when she wasn't worried. When she was younger, she used to get anxious on the school bus headed to school every morning, and she always felt swept away in the mass anxiety that was The Cafeteria in middle school and high school. Moving on to college, Kate's anxiety was replaced by a new friend: the buzz of alcohol helped ease her anxiety and nerves on dates and with new people.

After college and when partying wore thin, Kate noticed that her anxiety had become even more pronounced: she worried when getting on an airplane, worried that she wasn't doing well in her career, worried that she'd never find the right guy to marry. She also began to have really low times, when she felt like nothing mattered and wondered what the point of living was if she was always so worried.

When she met Jackson, Kate knew she loved him right away. He was just what she'd been looking for. Her anxiety and periods of self-doubt didn't go away after they met, however. They just started coming up in different ways. While planning their wedding, for example, she worried that something would go horribly wrong to humiliate her. Living together, she worried about some of Jackson's habits and began to doubt that he and she would ever find a way to be on the same page about the level of cleanliness in their home. She became anxious about their compatibility and their finances; she worried about their sex life. Just about everything seemed to present an opportunity for embarrassment, rejection, or failure.

When Kate became pregnant with their first child, she became distraught; she was overwhelmed and anxious about the future. When she tried to talk to Jackson about it, he didn't seem to understand. He took such a carefree attitude about everything. His laid-back attitude used to be attractive to her; she had loved the way he seemed so fearless and strong. But now she just felt frustrated. More than anything, she wanted Jackson to take her concerns seriously, so that they could address the issues together, but it seemed that every conversation with Jackson made her feel more frustrated.

Like Kate, you may have noticed that you tend to worry more than your partner does, and you may have experienced worry and anxiety in childhood. Sometimes, having waves of worry may be such a part of your everyday life that you don't even recognize it as anxiety—it just seems normal. But living with a partner and sharing your everyday concerns, you may find that your partner and you have very different levels of worry. It can feel frustrating to notice that something you care so much about seems inconsequential to your spouse.

A Demand/Withdraw Interaction

Intense feelings of worry from one partner can trigger what researchers call a *demand/withdraw interaction*. This interaction happens when one partner makes a complaint or requests a change, usually in the form of nagging, complaining, or criticizing. In response, the other partner avoids the request and withdraws from the conversation. Most frequently, women take on the demand role and men take the withdrawal role, particularly when the woman has chosen the topic of conversation (Heavey, Lane, and Christensen 1993). This demand behavior usually comes from strong emotions and frustration that your partner is failing to contribute or invest in the relationship (Sanford 2010). The demander is trying to influence some type of change in a situation found to be unfair or anxiety provoking. The more upset the demander, the more likely the conversation is to take on a coercive tone. The withdrawer, on the other hand, wants to avoid the issues, because he doesn't want to feel blamed or controlled and he anticipates that nagging or complaining will elicit these feelings (Sanford 2010).

For example, if Angela starts talking harshly with Jonathan, he's more likely to be reactive and to shut down fast. Angela feels empty and lonely, so she pushes for more contact. Jonathan feels criticized and withdraws. In this situation, both partners have strong emotional reactions and anticipate not getting their needs met. They both easily go into demand/withdraw mode when they see conflict coming.

While all couples may have the demand/withdraw interaction at times, couples who are distressed have the highest levels of this pattern (Baucom, McFarland, and Christensen 2010). A long-term effect of this pattern is that you and your partner may try to avoid talking about heated topics altogether or be reluctant to ask about how each other is feeling. This ends up alienating you from each other rather than making you closer. It also sets the stage for emotions to explode when the issues finally surface, for resentments may have been building. As upsetting as this pattern can be, it doesn't have to continue on in this way.

Breaking the Pattern

The demand/withdraw pattern is less likely to be activated when both of you are aware of the pattern, how it harms your relationship, and when you both make an effort to see how hard the pattern is for one another. In this way, having an honest conversation with your partner can be really helpful.

Additionally, if you notice that acting on the urge to make demands does more harm than good—that it will likely lead to more distance, not closeness—it's easier to resist the urge. Change sometimes starts with the recognition that your attempts to reduce your anxiety have actually become the source of your anxiety. Being able to approach your anxiety with emotional awareness, employing relaxation techniques such as deep breathing, and noticing your thoughts (see previous exercises) can help you handle worry before it places undue strain on your relationship.

When you recognize that you can only be responsible for your own behaviors and reactions, it allows space for you to accept that you can't always change your partner's feelings or way of handling a situation. Letting go of trying to control or change your partner can be very liberating. As you are able to monitor and be mindful of your own reactions to your partner, your reactivity will decrease. You will have less desire to demand change from your partner and instead will find a new level of peace, or acceptance for your own feelings, as well as acceptance for your partner.

The Fifty/Fifty Rule

In couples where one person is naturally more anxious or worried than the other, each half typically gets used to having an assigned, inflexible role. If you're the worrier in the relationship, your partner doesn't have to worry; you've got it covered. There's a level of homeostasis that's been established. Your partner may recognize (even unconsciously) that you will take care of something, so she doesn't need to fret about it. But when you reduce your amount of worry and investment in something, then your partner has more room to own her own portion of the concern. I call this shifting of balance, where you create more flexible roles, the *fifty/fifty rule*.

When you resist the urge to take the lion's share of concern about an issue in your relationship, your partner will naturally start to take ownership. For instance, a former client of mine, Jessica, tended to be the worrier in the relationship when it came to budgeting and finances. Her partner Reed tended to be the one who wanted to make more large purchases. They fell into a pattern where he was always coming to Jessica to ask permission to buy things, and she took on the role of budgeting gatekeeper. Jessica didn't really like this role—it made her feel like the perpetual parent in the relationship—so she decided to make some changes. She knew that she and Reed were fundamentally on the same page about how much to spend and how much to save for retirement, so when he would ask her for input about a big purchase, she began to encourage him to consider the outcomes and make the final decision for himself. Their dynamic began to shift. Rather than Reed coming to her to enforce a budget, he began to show more concern for saving.

You also can use the fifty/fifty rule to change the demand/withdraw dynamic. In this case, you need to think about how often you're approaching your partner for emotional involvement or support. If you are doing 90 percent of the reaching out, it can be nice to let your partner come to you instead. Recognize that by changing the dynamic and allowing your partner the space to reach out to you, you are deactivating the demand/withdraw pattern.

Now of course, you don't need to be fifty/fifty about everything. You may enjoy taking care of the garden while your partner likes paying the bills, for example. Alternatively, your partner and you may enjoy the fact that you're the more emotionally sensitive one who tends to bring up issues in your relationship. And certainly, when one of you is going through a really difficult time, it's natural for the other person to take on more responsibilities to help. But the fifty/fifty rule is a good way to think about remedying the areas of your relationship that feel routinely unbalanced.

When Worry Reduces Intimacy

What happens when you catch yourself worrying in the middle of spending quality time with your partner? On the one hand, you want to feel more connected to her. On the other hand, you're so worried about what's going wrong in the relationship or preoccupied with anxiety that you may fail to fully utilize or appreciate the time that you have together. Worry makes it hard to be fully present, and your partner can probably sense your discontent.

Turning your focus toward enhancing the connection to your inner experience and to your partner in the here-and-now is a powerful antidote to worry (Verplanken and Fisher 2013). Being fully present when you interact with your partner is one of the greatest gifts you can give to your relationship and to yourself.

Enhancing Your Connection

Imagine that you weren't able to see your partner for six months. How would it feel to be reunited? You would want to drink in every detail of her face, savor every touch, and listen intently to every word she says. In much the same way, focusing on being attuned to your partner helps you slow down and cherish the moment together.

Listening with attunement means that when your partner speaks, you take the time to really hear what he's saying. It's so easy to rush through a conversation or think ahead to the next topic. Instead, you can show that you're listening by asking questions about what your partner just said or by letting him know that you found his perspective interesting. When you speak to your partner, you can show that you're attuned by keeping your body language open—facing him, making eye contact, putting your hand on his hand or touching his shoulder in a tender gesture—any sign to show that you're there with him.

Tuning in with your five senses as you interact with your partner will help you be fully present in the moment.

Exercise: Tuning in with Your Senses

Try the following anytime you are with your partner and want to enhance the connection you have.

1. Begin by connecting to your present experience. Notice the details of your surroundings. Notice the fall leaves and crisp air surrounding you, the warm summer air, or the comfort of your home as you sit together with your partner.

2. Next, turn your attention to how you feel in your partner's presence. What does it feel like to be near him or her? If you're able to, reach out to hold your partner's hand or to walk arm and arm. Notice how it feels to have made a physical connection.

3. Now take a closer look at your partner and make eye contact. What reactions do you have to looking into your partner's eyes? How does your partner respond?

4. Tune into your sense of smell. What smells do you notice? Does your partner have a particular scent of perfume or aftershave? What's your reaction? What other smells do you notice? Perhaps it's fragrant flowers in the air, or the smell of a candle burning.

5. Listen with attunement. Pause after your partner finishes a sentence and allow the words to affect you. Think before you respond.

6. Speak with attunement. Consider the words you're using with your partner. Do your words accurately reflect what you're feeling on the inside? What does it feel like to talk with your partner?

    You'll notice that this exercise encourages you to approach your partner with a sense of wonder. Seeing the same person day after day can dull our sense of wonder and appreciation, whereas mindfulness reminds us of how unique each moment together really is.

Being tuned in to your partner also means recognizing that your partner is an evolving person. It's likely that your partner's opinions or perspectives may have shifted and evolved since the time you first met. Try to see your partner with new eyes. Ask questions about your partner's past. Ask her to tell you something that you don't already know about her. Let yourself be surprised and impressed by the partner you have before you.

Attunement doesn't mean that things are always happy or romantic. You can be attuned to someone who is upset; you simply acknowledge that the other person is in a bad place and allow there to be space for that. Being attuned to your partner and being mindful of your own reactions during stress can actually stop arguments from escalating. Most arguments or misunderstandings result from lack of attunement and awareness, so being more attuned will serve you well both in romantic connection and in difficult moments.

Practicing Gratitude

Practicing gratitude is another way to enhance your connection with your partner when worry has been getting in the way of intimacy. Feeling and expressing gratitude is a powerful antidote to fear and worry (Borkovec and Sharpless 2004). When you're depressed, it can initially be difficult to connect to feelings of gratitude, yet practicing loving-kindness can help foster those feelings. And research has shown that tuning into your feelings of loving-kindness can be one of the most healing, beneficial ways to improve your mood, relationships, and outlook on life (Emmons and McCullough 2003).

Exercise: Loving-Kindness Meditation

Begin a loving-kindness meditation by closing your eyes and remembering something that a friend, family member, or acquaintance did for you that made you feel happy inside.

Capture that feeling of warmth and happiness and send that feeling out into your entire body. As you do so, repeat a phrase to yourself, such as *May I be happy, may I find peace, and may I have joy.*

Now, take those feelings of gladness and silently send that energy out to a friend: *May you be happy, may you be healthy, and may you live with ease.*

Next, silently send that loving-kindness energy to a member of your family: *May you be loved, may you have peace, and may you live with ease.*

Now, spread the loving-kindness to your entire family: *May my loved ones be happy, peaceful, and free from suffering.*

Take a moment to reflect on the feelings of gratitude and peace that come with this practice of compassionate mindfulness.

Couples who practice gratitude interact with a heightened level of passion and awareness; they've made room for passion to enter into the relationship (Gordon et al. 2012). They refuse to take one another for granted, and they appreciate the interactions and special bond they have with their partners.

Exercise: Feeling Gratitude for Your Partner

Consider the following questions:

- What is it about your partner that makes him or her unique?

- What traits does your partner possess that make you smile?

- What traits do you most value and admire in your partner?

- When, in times of need, has your partner been there for you and supported you?

After pondering these questions, write down your answers in the following format:

- *I am grateful for my partner's unique traits. He is…*

- *I am grateful to my partner for making me smile when she…*

- *I admire and value in my partner his…*

- *I hold deep gratitude for the times she has supported me, such as…*

Afterward, take a few moments to close your eyes and reflect upon the feelings of gratitude and warmth you hold.

Another way of practicing gratitude is to look at your partner and allow your partner's features to remind you of qualities he or she possesses or of special moments you both have shared. For instance, looking into your partner's eyes, you might note that he has kind, loving eyes. Her smile might remind you of the caring, gentle way she plays with the kids. His shoulders might remind you of his strong embrace and how nice it feels to be the recipient of his caring protection. If doing this feels uncomfortable at first, remind yourself that it's okay to indulge in a little appreciation of your partner.

Exercise: Feeling Gratitude for Your Shared Past

To feel more connected to your partner, try doing some of the following. You may do these exercises on your own, or you may choose to involve your partner in the process.

- View an old photo album.

- Reread a book that you discovered with your partner many years ago.

- Revisit some favorite places from early in your relationship.

- Ask your partner about your first date—do you remember what were your first impressions?

- Recall those early stages of falling in love. How did it feel to have your first kiss? Did you try to impress each other? Allow yourself to laugh and be moved by these strong memories of being with your partner.

- Think back to the first vacation you took together. Where did you go? What happened on that first trip?

- Recall the time you first discovered your favorite restaurant together. What made it special?

- What are some of the most meaningful moments you've shared together in your home?

As you revisit special moments from the past, turn your attention to the feelings of warmth and gratitude that you feel in the present moment.

If you have ever lost someone you loved or have experienced hardship, you've learned a great lesson. The lesson is that it is all too easy to take for granted what we have. The people and things that make up our lives can change in an instant. We often spend our time wishing for more things—more possessions, a raise, a better job—and lose sight of what we have right in front of us. Maybe it's appreciating the dirty clothes that your partner left on the bedroom floor or the dirty dishes in the sink. Yes, it all needs to be cleaned up, but more than that, it represents a moment in time. Rather than thinking of picking these items up as a chore, you might choose to relish the memory of the dinner you enjoyed eating together or of what happened after the clothes came off.

Take a mental snapshot of the moment. Ten years ago, things were probably different in your life, and in ten more they will have changed again. There is something so sweet about appreciating life as it is exactly in this moment.

Conclusion

Mindfulness and attunement are skills that foster balance and interdependence. When you're more aware of your own emotions and needs, you're better able to manage your feelings and better able to meet the needs of your partner. Anxiety and worry tend to skew the balance of your relationship. They can make you overly concerned with the future or the past, leaving the present experience neglected. Mindfulness and acceptance of both your moods and a range of emotional experiences allow you to restore that balance.

As you recognize the underlying emotions related to your anxiety, also recognize that it's okay to need love and to want acceptance from your partner. If you need a hug, ask for one. If you need words of encouragement, let your partner know. The healthiest couples make decisions together, support one another emotionally, and have a certain level of interdependency.

By the same token, being supportive of your partner's needs is equally important. When you're feeling depressed, it might feel overwhelming to have to be attuned to someone else's needs. Yet it can be as simple as recognizing and respecting that he needs space, or paying attention to the way you interact when she comes to you for support.

The message to take from this is twofold. First, you need to be aware of how your depression and anxious attachment are related: you're more likely to have anxious feelings about your partner because you struggle with depression. It's helpful to remember that these anxious feelings have more to do with how you perceive the world than how devoted or committed your partner actually is to you. You can use the mindfulness skills you've learned in this chapter to turn your fear into an opportunity to grow more deeply connected to yourself.

Secondly, feeling connected is a healthy, vital part of loving someone. Without the desire to connect to your partner, it would be hard to maintain your relationship. Not every situation is going to be perfect, and it doesn't need to be. But small interactions do add up and play a big role in your overall satisfaction.

The key is to embrace as many moments of mindful connection as you can. It's about being in tune with your own thoughts and emotions, paying attention to your partner's wishes, helping your partner know how to understand your needs, and being responsive to his needs in turn. As you start employing the techniques of attunement, mindfulness, gratitude, and clear communication, you'll notice that you're allowing space for intimacy and feelings of closeness to flourish.

chapter 5

How to Feel Good Enough for Your Partner

Insecurity and feelings of low self-worth are major roadblocks to a healthy relationship. Research shows a strong relationship between self-worth and well-being in relationships (Murray et al. 2003). With low self-esteem and depression, you live under the constant strain of self-recrimination and fear of rejection. You may be pushing your partner away because you don't believe you deserve your partner or because you fear that your partner will see you as negatively as you see yourself: *Why would she want to be with me when she can have someone better? Am I a burden?* or *What does he see in me? It's only a matter of time before he gets tired and leaves me.* You may have experienced feelings of worthlessness, guilt, and hopelessness. These feelings often snowball into self-reprimands, where you end up feeling ashamed that you feel so badly about yourself. When you're in a great deal of pain, you may end up shutting out your partner and withdrawing to avoid being hurt further (Smith, Breiding, and Papp 2012).

"What's wrong with me? Why can't I just get over it?" These are words that I hear from countless people who are struggling with depression. This overarching feature of depression—the feeling that one's self, the essence of who you are, is somehow defective—is at the core of many people's view of themselves when they are depressed.

But you don't have to live your life judging, criticizing, and disliking yourself. Instead, you can focus on increasing self-compassion and kindness toward yourself. Finding ways to increase your compassion is linked to lower levels of depression (Leary et al. 2007) and higher levels of life satisfaction (Neff, Rude, and Kirkpatrick 2007) and increased connectedness (Neff 2003).

This chapter reviews the effect of low self-esteem on your relationship and gives you some tools to build your self-esteem. As you develop inner confidence and nourish the areas of your life that are most meaningful to you, you'll be better able to connect and relate to your partner.

Self-Esteem and Depression

Research shows a strong relationship between low self-esteem and depression. Namely, those who have low self-esteem are more vulnerable to becoming depressed (Sowislo and Orth 2013). Having problems with negative thoughts about yourself is often a long-standing issue that is present prior to your first depressive episode. Because the burden of feeling bad about yourself can cause so much distress, having low self-esteem ends up making you feel hopeless about your ability to change, influence, or affect your future.

Low self-esteem causes depression through several avenues that are related to your interactions with others. One research finding is that if you have low self-esteem, you're more likely to seek excessive reassurances from your friends and your partner, which can end up turning them off (Smith, Breiding, and Papp 2012). Because of this, it's helpful to practice emotional awareness and mindfulness (see chapter 4) to help you change a pattern of excessive reassurance-seeking.

Another finding is that when you have a low estimation of yourself, you may be more likely to seek out friends who will agree with—or *verify*—your negative self-view. Surrounding yourself with people who don't have a lot of respect for you, are unsupportive, or treat you poorly will make you feel rejected and alone. You're more likely to become depressed when you lack strong social support. Because of this, it's important to pay close attention to the people you surround yourself with and spend the most time with. If you end up feeling upset after most interactions with them, it may be time to invest in new friends who are more supportive.

How You See Yourself

Your self-perception has to do with your thoughts and views about yourself and how competent you generally feel. Your sense of self is shaped by your past experiences and the types of messages you received about your value, how family members treated you as you were growing up, and how you were treated by other kids in school and by the larger community.

Your self-perception also has to do with how well you believe you're able to cope with adversity or difficulties. When you have a strong sense of self-efficacy, you believe you can handle the difficulties life that sends your way. This shapes your beliefs about yourself and contributes to a feeling of being able to influence your own direction in life. When you struggle with low self-esteem, however, it feels like you're constantly disappointed in yourself and have little influence over your direction in life. You have trouble with identifying your good qualities.

If you've struggled with low self-esteem, you know it can be difficult to move past negative thoughts and feelings about yourself. You may have tried positive self-statements, affirmations, or positive mantras and found they don't always work. Thinking of yourself as *not good enough* may have become a part of your identity, so it feels like you're lying to yourself when you try to convince yourself that you feel otherwise. Alternatively, when you focus on your strengths, you may find that you do get a boost in how you feel about yourself, but it's only temporary because you're ignoring the root of the problem, which is accepting flaws within yourself.

While there is no silver bullet that will magically improve your self-esteem, you can approach the feelings that you have about yourself in more helpful ways. These include fostering self-compassion (Lincoln, Hohenhaus, and Hartmann 2013), working on self-acceptance, and living by your values (Hayes, Strosahl, and Wilson 1999), even in the face of making mistakes, feeling flawed, and being imperfect.

Fostering Self-Compassion

Self-compassion is about seeing yourself as *good enough* and treating yourself with kindness. Rather than evaluate yourself based on your body, your status, or job title, you can learn to appreciate the value that is inherent with simply being who you are. This means not grading, judging, or rating yourself on any external measure but rather learning to unconditionally accept yourself. Instead of denying or feeling ashamed about your flaws, you can learn to recognize that having flaws and dark moments is simply a part of the human experience.

Exercise: Describing Yourself Inside and Out

Begin with two clean sheets of paper and a pen or pencil.

On the first piece of paper, write down all of the traits and characteristics that other people would be able to see in you based on outward appearances. This list might include such specific details as your occupation or being a mom or dad, as well as language such as "kind," "generous," "stylish," or however others might see you.

On the second piece of paper, use different language to describe who you are on the inside—the traits that other people can't see. Be as honest as you can with yourself. No one will see this but you.

Now compare the two lists. What do you notice? There probably is not a 1:1 correlation between them. After all, we all have thoughts about ourselves that we keep to ourselves.

Here is something else to consider. As you were writing the second list, what was your experience? Was there any sense of shame? Confusion? Distress? Pride? Lastly, did you hear any other people chime in to the conversation? Were there internal voices from your past, repeating messages you heard about yourself growing up?

The mind is like a tape recorder, where you can almost hear what you imagine someone would say about you—or at some point really did say to you. These old tapes replay and add to your sense of self. If you did hear any of those tapes, what did they say? Who was speaking? And most importantly, do you believe what they said about you?

How others view you, or what the world sees from the outside, is often a gauge people use for their sense of self-worth. Unfortunately, seeking approval from others can be a superficial quest, since your sense of self can easily be diminished by one naysayer who views you negatively or criticizes your accomplishments. In this way, it's very difficult to build a sense of self-worth based on external markers. When you care too much about what others think about you, you're more vulnerable to feeling judged, devalued, and inferior.

It's more helpful to focus on how you view yourself on the inside. Look back at the list in the last exercise in which you described yourself based on who you are on the inside. This list is the one that holds more weight and is the core self you need to explore further. The next exercise will help you practice finding acceptance for yourself—including the parts of yourself that you may keep hidden or feel ashamed of, as well as the parts of which you're proud—through practicing compassion (Gilbert 2009).

Exercise: Listening to Yourself with Compassion

Use the powers of your imagination to conjure an image of a kind, compassionate person. Perhaps it's a loving grandmother or a teacher you had in school. It could be a person whom you've never met. It could even be a movie character.

Now take a look at all of the words on the second list that you used to describe yourself in the last exercise. With this compassionate person in mind, try to imagine what this person might say when viewing this list. What might she say about the struggles that you feel inside? How might he respond to the critical thoughts you have about yourself?

Allow yourself to fully experience the compassionate response that you imagine this person would give. What does it feel like to hear these kind words?

If you don't have a lot of experience being kind to yourself or receiving compassion from others, it can be really hard to imagine what a kind or compassionate person might say. A good example would be from the following conversation, in which two friends, Candice and Julie, debrief after Julie's speech at their alumni event:

Julie: That was so extremely stupid. I cannot believe I just spoke in front of all those people like that. Everyone thinks I'm an idiot.

Candice: Honey, it's okay. No one thinks you're an idiot. Everyone makes mistakes sometimes. Anyone who would judge you for that is not a good friend. So who cares what they think?

Julie: I care. Everyone saw me stumble and stammer. I got all red in the face and could hardly speak. It was a disaster. I froze like a deer in headlights.

Candice: And you also picked yourself up and got right back on track. I think that what felt to you like a century of silence was actually a minute or so.

Julie: I was humiliated. I'll never live it down.

Candice: Julie, you are not defined by one moment in your life. I don't think it's possible to go through life without stumbling a little bit. No one expects you to be perfect.

Julie: But I do!

Candice: It sounds like you're beating yourself up. It's so hard for me to see you being so tough on yourself. You had the courage to get up there and speak to that group of strangers, and that says something about your character.

Julie: Yes, I guess so. I was amazed that I was able to do it! And once I got going, it wasn't so bad. And people in the audience seemed interested and laughed at my humor. Afterward, they all said it was a great presentation.

Candice: I'm proud of you. It takes a lot of courage to do public speaking, and you did it even though it was difficult.

If you struggle with low self-esteem, you probably spend a lot of time focusing on aspects of yourself that you don't like. You may have self-critical thoughts that you tend to repeat over and over again, feeling helpless to make them stop, which can lead to isolation and withdrawal.

It's important to be on the lookout for those critical thoughts. When they emerge, you can counter them by picturing a compassionate person, as you did in the exercise, and reminding yourself gently of this compassionate perspective. You can also address your negative thoughts by realizing that they don't really set you apart from others and make you a failure. In fact, they make you better able to relate to others, because everyone has self-critical thoughts. Everyone feels bad sometimes. This is part of the human condition.

Instead of beating yourself up, it can be very healing to use your pain to find ways to relate to and have compassion for others (Dym 1996). Self-acceptance builds tolerance for others. Being aware of your own pain gives you the ability to understand how others may feel when they are experiencing hardship. By reaching out to someone who may need your help or understanding, you can use your compassion to make connections. Perhaps it's a coworker who's having a hard time or a student who needs mentoring. Perhaps it's finding a way to relate more to your own family, your spouse or your children, and focusing more on their well-being (Odegaard 1996). By connecting with and providing empathy for others, you're fostering the compassion, acceptance, and kindness inside of you.

Coping with Perfectionism

Many people who have perfectionistic traits do not think of themselves as perfectionists. When you think of a perfectionist in the traditional sense, you may imagine someone who has perfectly sharpened pencils lined up on his desk and never has wrinkles in his clothes. But perfectionism often looks very different from this and sometimes it's hard to see from the outside. Perfectionism is more about the critical voice that's inside—the inner critic.

With perfectionism, there is a drill sergeant inside of you who's never satisfied. You set standards for yourself that are far beyond reach or reason. And if you don't meet a certain standard—no matter how unrealistic or unattainable—you cannot tolerate the feeling of failure and embarrassment. Take a look at this list to see how many of these perfectionistic traits you see in yourself:

- *I often criticize myself for mistakes or small faults.*

- *I work hard to maintain a flawless image for others and care a great deal about how others perceive me.*

- *I find that I am second-guessing myself constantly.*

- *I feel embarrassed or ashamed by my weaknesses and want to hide my flaws from others.*

- *I sometimes feel that if people knew the real me, they would be disappointed.*

- *I easily dismiss my own achievements and concentrate on the flaws I see in myself.*

- *I become defensive when coworkers, friends, or employers give me feedback.*

- *I am fearful of making mistakes and worry that I won't do a good job.*

- *Feeling overwhelmed often gets in the way of my performance at work.*

- *I have the desire to always have the right answer and be perfectly knowledgeable.*

- *I tend to be rigid or inflexible with expectations of others and myself.*

When you notice the drill sergeant of perfectionism starting to emerge, you can employ a couple of strategies to refocus your energy.

Seek Growth, Not Perfection

When you think about people you greatly admire, what do you admire about them? What hardships have they endured? What mistakes have they made? Did they always have the right answer the first time, or have they always performed flawlessly? Likely, the answer is no. The people we admire most are often not those who are perfect but rather those who have overcome adversity.

In a similar way, you can think about times when you've struggled the most. What did you learn about yourself? How did you grow? During difficult times, it's helpful to ask yourself these questions. The key is to recognize that imperfection is part of what makes you an appealing, complex individual, and that you can learn from your setbacks.

People who achieve the most success in life are those who grow from their experiences. As you learn to look for the moments of self-reflection and growth that come along with so-called failures, you will recognize that you weren't really failing after all.

Seek Challenges, Not Perfection

If you set goals for yourself that are unrealistic, you may end up giving up. Your goals may feel so unattainable that they drain your motivation to try anything. But does that mean you should avoid setting goals? Not at all!

The answer is to challenge yourself while making space for self-compassion when you notice harsh thoughts coming up. Giving yourself permission to make mistakes can be quite liberating. You can say to yourself, *You have permission to be imperfect.* Or *My goal is to see this through, work my hardest, and be kind to myself throughout the process.*

Finding a way to challenge yourself may mean using skills that you already possess but pushing yourself to use them in a new way. For example, Tami noticed that she tended to sell herself short when it came to preparing for work presentations. She told me that her high standards tended to paralyze her, and she usually ended up procrastinating and underpreparing because she felt that no matter what she did, it would not be good enough.

Once she realized that aiming for perfection was getting in the way, Tami decided to set a new goal of working on her presentation for a half hour each day. By changing her goal, she challenged herself without the pressure of perfectionism.

Another client named Celina, who had always been athletic, decided to take her skills to the next level by running a marathon. While she enjoyed pushing herself to go faster, she reminded herself that the goal of running the marathon was not to have the fastest time, but to see it through, even when it was difficult. Crossing the finish line was a proud moment for her, representing a great deal of personal growth. Another client had always enjoyed playing music in school, so he decided to take guitar lessons. He found learning guitar to be a challenge and a great deal of work. It was intimidating to know how much effort it would take to become proficient, but he learned to take pleasure in small improvements and the sense of accomplishment that he felt after a long practice session.

Challenging yourself will help your relationship, as accomplishing new feats helps you feel more capable. By pushing your boundaries, you gain a sense of mastery. Regardless of the outcome, the fact that you've expanded your comfort zone contributes to your feeling of competence. You realize that you can stand on your own. For your relationship to feel healthy, it's important that you derive strength from within rather than only from your partner.

Living by Your Values

Another helpful strategy for building your sense of self-worth is to focus on making your life purposeful. People who live by their values report higher levels of happiness and well-being than those who search fruitlessly for happiness in other ways. Living by your values is also good for your relationship. The ability to be close and connected to your partner while still maintaining your individuality is an indicator of a strong relationship (Skowron 2000).

Making your life purposeful consists of asking yourself some key questions:

- *How can I create a life that I feel is worth living?*

- *What would a worthwhile, purposeful life look like?*

- *What matters most to me in life?*

- *What do I want to be remembered for by the people I love?*

- *What are my dreams for the future?*

Your values act as a beacon for your direction in life, guiding you toward personal fulfillment. They give meaning and inspiration to your life. Remembering your values helps you break out of depression by reminding you of the path you wish to travel and by helping you to connect with others along this path. Examining your values is a core component of acceptance and commitment therapy for depression (Hayes, Strosahl, Wilson 1999).

Exercise: Examining Your Core Life Values

Find a quiet place and give yourself enough time to complete this exercise thoughtfully. Follow these steps:

1. Take a moment to think about these areas of your life: recreation and fun, family or raising children, spirituality, friendship and social activities, career and education, intimacy and affection with your partner, money or financial success, creativity, autonomy and independence, culture/arts, nature, altruism or helping others, physical activity. Which of these areas are more important to you? Which are less important? The areas of life that are the most important reflect your core values.

2. Now list each of these areas of your life in their order of importance to you. First on your list should be the area that you value the most, second on the list is the area that you value second-most, and so on until you've listed all of the areas that you value according to the order in which you value them. (A downloadable worksheet is also available for you to use in completing this activity; visit http://www .newharbinger.com/28326 to access it, or see the back of this book for more information.)

3. Evaluate how you fulfill each of these areas. What activities do you engage in? Which areas are being most fulfilled right now? Which areas would you like to develop?

4. Now come up with a different list showing how much time you currently spend on each of these areas. What should come first on this list is the area that you spend the most time on, second is the area that you spend the second-most time on, and so on until you've listed all the areas of importance in your life according to how much time you spend on them.

    How does this list compare with your first list? Is there a discrepancy between what you'd prefer to be doing and what you actually are doing in your life? Perhaps you ideally value family time, showing intimacy and affection to your loved ones, but find that realistically most of your time is being spent at work. The closer you can align your values to your actions, the more fulfilled you will feel.

5. Now think of a time when have you felt the most aligned with your core values. Who were you with, what were you doing, and what was your state of mind? What motivated you at the time?

6. Identify one to three core values that you would like to develop more in your life. What steps might you take to do this? What would it look like, specifically, if you were actively engaged in living your life with these values in mind?

7. Commit to implementing these core values in your life. Make a written commitment, sign up for a class, or tell a friend. Find a concrete way to show your commitment to these values.

Bringing your life more into alignment with your own values can be a powerful way out of depression. Having made a commitment to pursue areas you value helps you tolerate the distress that comes with life, making difficult times easier to work through. The more in line your actions are with your inner values, the greater your sense of direction and purpose.

The values you hold may focus your time and efforts toward pursuits without your partner, and that's okay. Having your own interests and passions can strengthen your connection to your partner. This is because a sense of autonomy builds confidence. Feeling good is not dependent on your partner or an outside source; it stems from within. When you feel good about yourself in this way, you're able to support your partner's endeavors without feeling abandoned or left behind. Instead, you find that having your own pursuits helps you feel closer to your partner when you come back together.

In addition to developing your own values, you can also look for ways you can incorporate your values into your time as a couple. Addison and her fiancé Craig discussed their shared goals and realized they both valued their shared Italian culture and heritage. They decided they would take an evening course learning to speak

Italian and work toward planning a trip to Italy. Another couple, David and Carrie, realized that they both valued their Christian upbringing and decided to attend church together more regularly. You may talk to your partner and find that you want to volunteer together, start saving toward traveling together, or expand your social circle. You could take a weekend course on starting your own business or take an art course together.

Finding Joy in Daily Life

Do you ever wake up and feel listless and empty, unsure of what you want to do? Sometimes, it may feel like bridging the gap between how you want to live and your actual daily life is difficult to do. You may feel a lack of energy or have difficulty finding motivation. A common roadblock for depression in relationships is when you have difficulty clarifying which activities you find really fulfilling, either with or without your partner. You may end up staying home and isolating yourself, which causes you to sink deeper into depression.

The technique of behavioral activation is an evidence-based treatment for depression that looks at the function of your daily activities and how they affect your mood (Martel, Addis, and Dimidjian 2004). It helps you consider:

- How do you spend most of your days?

- Which of your daily activities make your depression worse?

- Which activities help you feel better?

By simply noticing which activities lead you to feel better and then doing those activities more regularly, you can help beat the blues. As simple as this sounds, we often don't take the time to closely track how we spend our time or to pay attention to how our feelings are related to daily activities.

The reason this is so helpful to your relationship is that improving your mood helps you feel more positive and engaged with your partner. It helps you feel a sense of purpose and passion each day. As a bonus, evaluating how to best spend your time helps you look at how much time you need to spend alone versus with your partner. Different people have varying levels of time they need to spend on their own to recharge. Some people may find that their car ride home from work in the afternoon fulfills their requirement for alone time, whereas others may find that they need an afternoon each weekend to swim or bike on their own.

This next exercise helps you to identify your regular activities and to monitor how your mood changes when you engage in different ones. To get the most out of this exercise, you will need to devote at least a week to paying attention to how you spend your time.

Exercise: Assessing How Your Mood Relates to Your Activities

Take a moment to think about all your different activities. Using this list as a guide, write down examples of activities that you do, making note of when, where, and for how long you do each activity.

- **Activities or hobbies you do on your own,** such as journaling, reading, taking a walk, or painting

- **Family activities** or time with your children, such as going to the park, playing board games, playing sports, or reading together

- **Activities with friends,** such as talking on the phone, attending a book club, or hosting a dinner party

- **Recreation activities,** such as doing hobbies or engaging in sports

- **Career and work activities,** such as finishing a project, getting a new client, or earning praise for your accomplishments

- **Intimacy and affection** with your partner, including cuddling, making love, giving massages, and holding hands or hugging

- **Rest and relaxation,** including your sleep schedule (noting the time you wake up each day, what time you go to bed, how many hours you sleep, and if you have a regular sleep schedule or not) and leisure activities, such as reading or yoga

- **Food and eating habits,** such as how your prepare food, if you eat out, what foods you eat, how frequently you eat or snack, and if you eat alone or with others

- **Spirituality or personal development,** such as attending a religious ceremony, meditation, creating artwork, or journaling

For one week, keep a daily activity log focusing on these different areas. Immediately after you complete each activity, rate your mood on a scale of 1 to 5, where a rating of 1 means you feel very depressed or discontent, 2 means you feel somewhat depressed, 3 means you feel neutral or just okay, 4 means you feel somewhat pleased, energized, satisfied, or content, and 5 means you feel very content, pleased, energized, or satisfied. (A downloadable worksheet is available at http://www.newharbinger.com/28326 for you to complete this activity. See the back of this book for more information.)

Example:

Category	Activity	Length of Activity	Mood Rating
Family	Swimming with the kids	2-3:30 p.m. 1.5 hours	4

After at least a week of rating your moods, take a look at which activities put you in the best moods. Perhaps you felt great after spending family time and showing intimacy and affection to your loved ones. Perhaps you found that you felt pleased and satisfied at work right after you completed a major project.

Imagine how you might rearrange your current schedule to make time to engage in the activities that you like the most. What changes could you make to your schedule today? What long-term changes might you make?

Note the activities that you consistently liked doing the least, or where you felt depressed after doing them. Think about ways you can reduce how much you do these activities in your life. For instance, if you found that eating alone resulted in a low mood, make an effort to schedule lunch with a friend three days a week. If you found that you feel bad after getting less than six hours of sleep, make it a priority to get seven to eight hours of sleep.

What you may notice is that certain activities that you don't think of as making you feel better actually do. Maybe you feel really good after taking the dog on a walk, even though sometimes you dread walking the dog. The idea of walking the dog may not inspire you, but the effect of taking the walk feels really good. Afterward, you're energized and have a sense of contentment. Similarly, finishing up a difficult work project might rank high because there's a sense of pride that comes with completing a difficult task.

Continuing to pay attention to what improves your mood and gives you satisfaction is key to reducing the risk of periods of depression in the future. Make it a habit to check in with yourself regularly. Your relationship with your spouse will benefit from your effort to do more activities that boost your mood. Good moods are contagious. The more time you spend on pleasurable, satisfying endeavors, the more that pleasant feelings will follow. And that will do wonders for your love life.

Sharing Good Times with Your Partner

Sometimes you may be at a loss for how to spend time with your partner when you have free time together. Your mood will benefit from being active, even if you don't initially feel highly motivated. Here are some ideas to get you started.

Bake a cake together from scratch.

Go to a sports game together and root for the same team.

Go to a music concert.

Plan a trip together to visit a place you've always wanted to go.

Have a candlelit dinner for two at home.

Go bowling.

Play miniature golf.

Watch the sunset together.

Go kayaking.

Put on your favorite kind of music and have a dance party together.

Look through your favorite photos together.

Go to the zoo.

Plan a date at the same place where you had your first date.

Go to a race.

Go shopping together.

Watch Carl Sagan's series *Cosmos: A Personal Voyage* together and discuss it.

Go for a walk in nature.

Stroll through an outdoor art gallery.

Have coffee at a café and watch the world go by.

Volunteer together.

Play hide-and-seek.

Go hiking and have a picnic.

Join a couples book club, or read the same book at the same time.

Go to a comedy show.

Play a board game.

Play cards.

Go garage-sale hopping.

Go to your place of worship together.

Snuggle up together on a weekend morning.

Go wine tasting.

Take a bath together.

Explore a new city together.

Sing karaoke together and dedicate a song to each other.

Pick out plants and flowers for your garden and plant them together.

Celebrate an anniversary.

Go fly-fishing.

Take a drive someplace new.

Walk the dogs together.

Wash the car together.

Take turns giving each other massages.

Play a video game together.

Buy painting supplies and paint a room together.

Collect something from nature together (starfish, flowers, shells).

Decorate a space together; make it your special room in the house.

Have a quiet dinner together, turning off all electronics and avoiding interruptions.

Watch the sunrise together.

Tell each other about your favorite childhood memories.

Play outside in the snow/leaves/sunshine/rain.

Tell each other about your greatest dreams and aspirations.

Plan a trip together to revisit the place you went on your honeymoon.

Make a date for ten years from now. What would you like to be doing together?

As you engage in an activity with your partner, use the skills of mindfulness, attunement, and gratitude to be fully present. The way you interact together is just as important, if not more, than what you choose to do together.

It also can be really nice to plan a calendar together or sync your electronic calendars for common activities. Doing this helps to ensure that you carve out time for each other and follow through on your commitments.

Conclusion

Committing to living your life in a meaningful way and filling your day with moments of joy are wonderful ways to change how you feel about yourself. As you engage in new activities, notice the compassion you feel toward others you encounter. How does it feel?

Embracing who you are—all aspects of yourself—is a powerful way out of depression, as your autonomy and sense of identity provide feelings of strength that will help you feel capable and fulfilled. When you have feelings of shame or feel disappointed in yourself, remember that those moments don't make you any less of a good person. In fact, they add to your ability to be a caring, compassionate, well-rounded person. It's good to remember to love yourself even when you're discouraged and to be kind to yourself when it's most difficult, because those are the moments when you most need self-compassion.

chapter 6

Reigniting Your Sexual Desire

Bethany and Nick had been married for nine years. They told me that during the first few years of their marriage, they were madly attracted to each other. They fell into a routine of having good sex, and both were pleased with the amount and frequency of their sex life. Then, two years ago, Nick was laid off from his job when his company was bought out. He spent the next eight months looking for a job, and his severance package was about to expire. With the stress of looking for a job in a tight market, his interest in sex became almost nonexistent. Bethany had a stable job, and they were able to get by on her income, but it was clear that Nick didn't feel good about himself or his position. He wanted to contribute financially. He also lost the sense of identity that had come with his career. He began having doubts about his self-worth.

Bethany knew that Nick was going through a period of depression, but they didn't talk about it openly. Bethany tried to connect with Nick by being supportive but also by giving him space. Nothing seemed to help. She worried that he somehow resented her. As he fell into depression, he began isolating himself from her, both physically and emotionally. When she tried to initiate sex, he showed little interest. When they did have sex, it felt mechanical and empty. At first she was patient and didn't take his actions personally. But eventually she couldn't help but feel hurt and resentful. She was confused, thinking to herself, *Why is he turning away from me? I'm not the one who fired him from his job. If anything, I'm the most supportive person he has, and I'm the only one earning an income. How did I become the bad guy?* She stopped initiating sex, and the couple grew more distant.

When Nick found a new job, his mood gradually lifted. However, the couple's sex life didn't return. Nick immersed himself in his career, and Bethany continued to feel resentful that he never acknowledged how he had treated her during the period when he had no job. By the time they came to me for counseling, both expressed concern that their sexual desire for one another was nonexistent. They hadn't had sex in over four months. Nick said that when he reached out to Bethany, she was unreceptive. Bethany said that she felt like a switch had been turned off, and she felt no desire at all for Nick. In fact, sex was the last thing she wanted.

Many couples where one partner or both partners are struggling with depression also have problems with their sex life. When depression gets in the way of your sex life, your relationship bond doesn't have a chance to grow. Part of your relationship has been starved, and that absence seeps into other areas of your life. The reasons couples don't have sex may vary, but the common denominator remains: a lack of intimacy and sex will cause you to feel alienated from one another. While a lack of sexual connection has serious repercussions for your relationship's stability and well-being, the opposite is also true; having a good sex life accounts for 15 to 20 percent of satisfaction in healthy relationships (McCarthy and McCarthy 2003).

This means that for happy couples, sex is a fulfilling and vital part of their lives. On the other hand, couples in distress almost always have problems in the sexual department (McCarthy and McCarthy 2003).

Having periods of less interest in sex is fairly normal. In the case of Nick and Bethany, it was understandable that they might have a lull in their sex life while they worked out their career concerns. Similarly, if you and your partner experience a period of intense stress and change with, say, a home-renovation project—with dust flying all over the house and meals being consumed on the go, along with the usual demands of work and parenting—it is safe to say that sex may not be your top priority. But what if your lack of desire for sex feels like more than just a temporary lull? When it becomes more than just a down period, and it doesn't feel like a passing phase, it's time to look at other reasons for why your sex drive may have diminished.

Depression and Your Sex Drive

Both men and women can experience low sex drive due to depression. Whether it's an inability to become aroused, lack of interest in sex, tiredness or fatigue, feeling guilty, erectile dysfunction, or an inability to reach orgasm, depression may be interfering. And unless the sexual issues in your life are addressed, they can cause your relationship to suffer and break down, even after the period of depression has passed.

Low libido is the most common sexual problem couples experience (Beck 1995). Seventy-five percent of people who are depressed report a lack of sex drive. Because sex is so important to your relationship, this chapter will introduce some reasons why people experience low libido and give you some ideas for how to address this problem if it applies to you. It will help you reinvest in your sexual relationship and give you some new tools to develop your sexual energy.

Common Sexual Concerns

Low libido when you are depressed can come from a number of different sources: unexpressed emotional pain and resentment; guilt and shame about sex; poor body image; feelings of fatigue or tiredness; physiological problems; and misconceptions about technique—all are common concerns.

Emotional Pain and Resentment

If your sexual desire has waned, it's likely that both you and your partner have noticed and felt its effect on your relationship. In the case of Bethany and Nick, it became clear that they needed to talk about what had happened with their sex life, so they could move forward in their marriage. Their emotional attachment had been hurt by their sexual detachment. As they discussed the turmoil of the past few years, Nick explained that his lack of desire during that time had nothing to do with Bethany. If anything, he had experienced self-loathing during his unemployment, and it had been hard for him to feel desire or to imagine that Bethany truly desired him. His masculinity had been tied to his ability to provide and contribute financially to the family. Without those contributions, he thought he was less appealing to her. Bethany talked about how she had felt rejected, both emotionally and physically, by Nick. She had blamed herself for his distance and begun thinking of herself as a failure.

Once they explained what they'd each been going through, they had an opportunity to clear up the misunderstandings that were keeping them apart. Nick told Bethany that he found her highly desirable. He realized that he needed to have self-worth to feel deserving of a wife as stable, loving, and caring as she was. In turn, she told him that she loved him regardless of his financial status. She let him know that she found him just as sexy as the first day they met—if anything, more so—now that she saw how strong he was in the face of adversity. They both realized that they had missed their sexual connection. When their relationship improved, so did their sex life.

As you can see with Bethany and Nick, not talking about your pain can breed resentment and extinguish your sex drive, and you may not realize that resentment has been playing a big role in this area. To address the role of resentment in your relationship, think about when you started feeling less interested in sex. Did it coincide with feeling hurt by your partner? Feeling abandoned or left to fend for yourself? Or feeling taken for granted? Have you felt that your partner has stopped making an effort to be romantic or to show affection toward you, and instead it feels that any touch you receive is a demand for sex? Do you often feel criticized or marginalized by your partner? These are core issues that must be addressed if you want to restore you sexual connection.

Prolonged feelings of anger can lead to resentment. Resentment can be sneaky but powerful. As much as you might try to ignore it or push it away, resentment can rear its head through your sexuality, or lack of sexuality (Beck and Bozman 1995).

Feeling like your spouse doesn't pay enough attention to you—or has mistreated you—can make you feel less than amorous (Hiller 2006). But once you identify what incidents may have caused you to feel resentful, it's helpful to talk to your spouse about the problem. Communicating helps you clear the air. When your spouse doesn't get the chance to know what has hurt you, he is robbed of the chance to make it better. Similarly, he needs to be able to let you know how he's feeling, and you need to hear his needs as well. Talking to your partner openly can have a large effect on your sexual satisfaction as well as your satisfaction relationship (Byers 2005). As Bethany and Nick discovered, working through your emotional issues together can help you reestablish your sexual desire for your partner.

Guilt and Shame About Sex

Sometimes a lack of desire has less to do with your partner and more to do with how you feel about yourself. Guilt and shame are major features of depression and can put a damper on your ability to embrace your sexuality.

Part of the problem is how we are socialized to think about masculinity and femininity. It's hard not to be surrounded by sex.

The movies graphically depict sexual acts. The entertainment industry is filled with beautiful women who strut around, barely clad in revealing outfits; and masculinity is often portrayed as men with bulging biceps, who have a permanently lusty demeanor and crave emotionless sex. Young men are socialized to sexualize women's bodies, to compete for women, to seek validation through sexual conquests, and to fear that talking about emotions is unmanly (Elder, Brooks, and Morrow 2012). But the reality is that as men age, they may need more stimulation and arousal to get and maintain an erection, and this can threaten your sense of masculinity unless you know that it's a normal process.

Similarly, sexualizing women can cause internal conflict when you are in a committed relationship. It may be difficult to reconcile yourself to the idea that your hot girlfriend is now the mother of your children, and you may feel less attracted to her than before. Integration of the two ideas—seeing your wife as hot and sexy while also seeing her as the mother of your children—is critical for your love life.

Women, in turn, are socialized to believe that to be feminine is to be caring, sensitive, nurturing, and warm. If you're a woman, your feelings of sexuality, aggressiveness, and lust may conflict with your sense of identity as a mother, caregiver, or nurturer. If you have sex before you're married, you may be labeled as promiscuous. Our culture tends to objectify women as sex objects and then relegate them to the nurturing, motherly role once past a certain age.

When young women are exposed to unrealistic mixed messages, these messages can cause distress. On the one hand, you're told that your worth is based on your ability to be sexually attractive, but on the other hand you're made to feel ashamed if you act on your sexual desire. The resulting guilt and confusion can suppress your natural feelings of sexual desire and inhibit the development of your sexuality.

A lack of authenticity in your sexuality can come from being surrounded by so much sex in the media. For both men and women, there's a way in which sex can become about what you're supposed to do, or what you're supposed to look like, or about following an ideal. For women concerned about matching the media's ideal of a tall, thin, shapely female figure, anything that differs may cause feelings of inferiority. For men, the size of your penis and your ability to perform in bed can preoccupy you. Either way, the authentic power of sex can get lost.

You may carry with you a sense of guilt from negative messages about sex or masturbation that you received while growing up. Sexual abuse or exploitation in childhood can cause guilt, as can contracting an STD at any point or having an abortion due to an unwanted pregnancy. You may have had negative sexual encounters or experiences in the past. Unexamined feelings can become overwhelming and can lead to depression. Feeling a disproportionate amount of guilt is part of depression; you may punish yourself and shut down sexually. You may need to address an unresolved trauma to release feelings of undue burden and guilt.

You may struggle with feeling guilty about your sexual functioning: *I don't have strong enough desire. I worry I'm inadequate. There's something wrong with me.* These guilty thoughts can interfere not only with your ability to enjoy sex but also with your desire for sex. As sex becomes a trigger for feeling guilty or ashamed, you may develop sexual inhibitions, and your desire for sex will diminish.

This next exercise can help you identify negative, self-critical thoughts that you may have about sex and replace them with healthy, compassionate views on your sexuality.

Exercise: Embracing Sex Without Guilt or Shame

Think of any negative beliefs that you have about yourself and your experience of sex, and write them down. Such beliefs often come in the form of feeling that you should be doing something that you're not doing or that you shouldn't be the way you are. Here are some examples.

- *I feel ashamed of my body during sex.*

- *I shouldn't feel this way about sex.*

- *I should look a certain way in order to be sexy.*

- *I should be able to relax, but my mind won't allow my body to enjoy the experience.*

- *There's something wrong with me if I fail to become aroused.*

Next, look at when these thoughts occur, and try to approach your beliefs with openness. What is happening in these moments? Here are some examples:

- *I notice myself feeling self-critical when my mood is low.*

- *I feel worried I'm not satisfying my partner.*

- *I feel selfish when I think I should be focused on my other responsibilities rather than sex.*

Next, find an accepting, alternative way to approach your inner experience. Identify the feelings you're experiencing, notice what judgment might be tied to those feelings, and try to suspend those judgments. When you notice the critical or fearful voice inside of you, respond with compassion. Here are some examples:

- *I will choose to focus less on having a perfect body and more on enjoying my sexual experiences.*

- *I know my partner is very sexually satisfied.*

As you move away from self-judgment, you can approach your sexual relationship with a greater sense of compassion, acceptance, and flexibility. When released from the prison of self-criticism, you have freedom to enjoy a more open and spontaneous sexual relationship.

Poor Body Image

How comfortable are you with your physical shape? Our bodies can be a source of shame and frustration. Poor body image can lead you to feel less interested in sex. For example, Marta had gained weight over the past five years. She talked about how she was pain-fully aware of the extra weight—her clothes fit tighter and she felt less attractive—but she also felt unable to stop her weight from getting even more out of control.

Over the same period of time, her sex life with her husband Edward had gradually decreased. Marta just didn't feel terribly sexy, and the weight made her feel self-conscious and less desirable.

Her body frequently came up when the issue of sex was on the table. "I just feel fat," she'd say, looking down at her thighs. "I don't feel sexy."

Edward tried to say the right thing: "Look, I love the way you look. I think you look beautiful."

But she would respond, "You're just saying that. Thank you, but I think you just say that to make me feel better. I look awful."

What was most upsetting is that Edward did find her beautiful. He loved the way her curves looked and felt, loved her soft and perfumed skin. His only regret was that his wife didn't feel desir-able. He wanted more than anything for Marta to feel wanted and to be able to accept his advances. Sometimes, he thought about how nice it would be if she would just reach out to him, initiate contact, and show him that she desired him.

Marta felt so insecure with her physical body that it had the effect of cutting her off from the sexual side of herself. She didn't realize that she had stopped initiating sex or realize that her partner was feeling unwanted.

Marta decided that the amount of time she spent feeling unhappy about her body and her sex life was taking too great a toll. She decided to invest some of her energy in becoming more fit and healthy rather than spending all of it wishing things were different. Taking care of herself by exercising, eating well, and spending some time on her appearance allowed her to be more accepting of her body and to feel more comfortable in her sexuality.

Self-care and grooming are important to your body image, and neglecting yourself takes its toll. Depression can be accompanied by problems with keeping up personal hygiene, like forgetting to wash your hair or to wear fresh clothes or to brush your teeth. Putting some effort into your appearance is important psychologically, because you are sending the message to yourself that you are worth it. A spray of cologne, getting a manicure, or wearing a new scarf can feel really good. Without going too far in the other direction—feeling that you need to always wear makeup or to be dressed in a suit to be sexy—taking care of your appearance can help your confidence. And getting exercise and keeping a healthy weight is another way to take care of yourself.

Feeling Tired and Fatigued

A busy life, when you're very focused on work and other duties, depletes your energy and can contribute to depression. When you're depressed, it's difficult to have enough energy to exercise; lack of exercise can result in unhealthiness, and also make you feel more depressed. In a circular fashion, when your body doesn't feel healthy, it's difficult to have the energy or the drive for sex. On the other hand, increasing exercise has shown a clear link to increased libido. Even taking a brisk walk for a half hour a day can work to improve your mood and your libido.

Depression and stress can also affect your sleep, and not getting enough sleep will also hurt your libido. The average person needs more than six hours; without this much sleep, you become chronically sleep deprived. In much the same way, sleeping too much can cause you to feel groggy and fatigued. One of the best ways to help with the problem of sleep is to set a schedule for sleep, making sure that you get about seven to eight hours. Once you have a routine in place, you'll notice how much better you feel.

Similarly, having kids can affect your energy level and cause fatigue. For new mothers, after the birth of your child, you will be focused on your child and your role as caretaker. You are likely sleep deprived, may experience weight gain, and will certainly feel overworked and exhausted. It may feel like the last thing you have time or energy for is sex with your partner. Sex feels like another chore on the to-do list, and that's if sex even makes it onto the to-do list. But as you will see throughout this discussion, making time for sex remains one of the keys to inviting your sexual energy to emerge.

Physiological Problems

There's no doubt that a mind-body connection exists between your mental health and your physical functioning. This means that your depression lowers your physical desire, and your physical desire (or lack of it) affects your depression. Meanwhile, certain physiological problems may be affecting both your physical desire and your depression.

Hormonal Changes

Hormones play an important role in the biological aspect of sexual desire and arousal. Specifically, testosterone has been found to be a key hormone involved in both male and female sexual functioning. Hormonal changes associated with menopause or having a baby are also linked to low sex drive and depression. Because of this, if you've experienced a change in your libido, you may want to see your doctor to evaluate any physiological causes. If you are a man and are experiencing problems with your erection, you may want to consult a urologist. For women with vaginal pain or arousal difficulties, it's best to consult a gynecologist or endocrinologist, or and individual specializing in sexual medicine.

Using Antidepressants

Medications you may be taking for depression can unfortunately have the side effect of lowering your libido. In addition, your SSRI could cause other sexual side effects like inability to achieve orgasm, erectile dysfunction, and delayed ejaculation (Phillips and Slaughter 2000). The side effects of the medication can last even after your depression has lifted. In this case, it may be helpful to discuss alternative medications with your doctor. It's also helpful to understand that your sexual-response system may take longer if you're on antidepressants, allowing you to have more patience with the process of becoming aroused.

Alcohol and Drugs

Alcohol and drugs are sometimes used as self-medication for depression because of their numbing effects on emotions. Many times, however, using substances as an escape ends up creating more problems than you had to begin with. Particularly, in regard to sexual functioning, both alcohol and drugs can cause you to have lower sexual arousal and desire. While a small amount of alcohol may enhance your arousal, too much will certainly lower your libido. One or two drinks can help some people feel relaxed and aroused, but overuse is something to be aware of when you're struggling with depression and low sex drive.

Performance Anxiety

If you've had problems with arousal or erection problems in the past, you may inadvertently put more pressure on yourself to perform well, as you may fear having another incident. When your focus during sex is solely on being able to reach orgasm or being able to keep your erection, you may find yourself completely distracted. This type of heightened pressure usually has the effect of reducing desire. You may have trouble enjoying the sensations and experiences that come with having sex. Instead, you're focused on evaluating or judging yourself. To counter this tendency, it's helpful to approach sex in a more relaxed and even playful manner. It's better simply to focus on enjoying the sensations and the feeling of being with your partner.

The next exercise encourages you to focus on what's happening while you make love. Using the skills of mindfulness, you can slow down and appreciate how your senses can be heightened.

Exercise: Approaching Sex with Mindfulness

Mindful awareness can begin long before you get into bed. You may want to spend some time caressing or holding your partner and then progress to foreplay.

As you caress your partner, notice the feeling of your partner's skin against your own skin. Embrace the pleasure that comes from your partner's touch.

Pay attention to your breath and changes to your body as you touch one another. What changes do you notice inside of yourself? What changes do you notice as you touch your partner?

Increase your awareness of how it feels to kiss. What sensations do you notice?

Pay attention to how your body feels and what emotions you encounter during and after this exercise. There is no right or wrong way to feel. Instead, try to simply take note of how you feel, and notice your reactions to being sensual with your partner.

By approaching sex mindfully in this way and by being more in the moment, you can counter your tendencies to worry.

Misconceptions About Sexual Technique

When the sex that you're having is not satisfying, it can lower your desire for sex, and low sexual desire can lead to relationship problems and depression. We assume that great sex should naturally happen when two people are in love. But the truth is that having a satisfying sexual relationship takes education about sexual technique, communication with your spouse, and experimentation.

My clients Theresa and Tom told me they had had a lot in common when they met. They connected as friends, first and foremost, and sexual feelings developed later in their relationship.

Despite their sexual attraction toward each other, they both secretly felt that something was missing from their sex life. Theresa struggled with being fully open and honest about what she wanted with her partner, because she felt embarrassed and ashamed to talk about what she liked. She wasn't sure if she even knew what she liked. Often, she felt that sex went from zero to sixty and was over before she could really get comfortable. Meanwhile, Tom felt that Theresa didn't enjoy their sex life as much as he did, and he even tried to get it over with quickly, hoping to accommodate her.

For Theresa, a critical first step was for her to explore her own sexual energy. Her sexuality was something that she hadn't spent a great deal of time thinking about. Yet she wanted to be able to express herself sexually and have that connection with Tom. She began by exploring her own sexual needs and desires through masturbation. By knowing her own body, she was able to teach Tom what felt best for her. Then Tom and she began experimenting with different types of touch. Both of them were better able to convey to one another what they found pleasing.

The following exercises are ways you can explore various types of touch with your partner. These focus on increasing sensual awareness of touch and experiences with your partner, without focusing on a particular goal of intercourse or orgasm.

Exercise: Taking a Sensual Shower Together

Start by gently removing one another's clothing and taking a moment to look at one another in the mirror. Part of the benefit of this exercise is being comfortable with your bodies together. Take a few moments to look at yourself and your partner with kind, accepting appreciation.

Next, begin by soaping up your partner in the shower and caressing him or her as you do so, gently, and then move onto washing her hair.

Next, allow your partner to wash you with soap, using gentle, soft motions, and to wash your hair.

After showering, take a moment to take turns drying one another off with gentle strokes. Wrap your partner in a towel and allow your partner to do the same for you.

This next exercise you can do with your partner to increase your sensual awareness with each other. Again, the focus is on experiencing a new way to touch one another, without the pressure of sexual intercourse or orgasm.

Exercise: Increasing Your Sensual Awareness

Begin after both of you are showered and clean, and you've created a quiet, calm atmosphere in your bedroom.

Have your partner lie face up with eyes open or closed, whichever feels most comfortable. This can be done naked or in a state of partial undress, whichever your partner prefers.

Begin to massage your partner, moving from the upper body to the stomach and down to the arms, thighs, calves, and feet. Avoid direct genital stimulation, but feel free to explore every other area of the body.

Vary your pressure, from soft to firm, and use different strokes such as light touch, circular motions, kneading motions, or long, deeper strokes.

Ask your partner to give you feedback about which sensations are most enjoyable and what types of touch feel most pleasurable.

Next, use your mouth to kiss and explore your partner's body, again moving from top to bottom. Be creative and continue to get feedback about which types of touch are desirable.

Now have your partner turn over, and repeat the process from head to toe, as your partner lies comfortably and continues to give you feedback about what feels good.

Next switch roles, allowing your partner to give you a sensual massage with hands and mouth, so you can share what feels best to you.

Lie with your eyes open or closed, whichever you feel most comfortable with. Your partner should vary the pressure, speed, and type of touch, using hands, lips, and tongue.

Turn on your stomach and allow your partner to massage you sensually on every part of your body.

These exercises offer a safe, relaxed environment to explore what feels good to you. As you explore what types of touch you enjoy, you can continue to communicate with your partner about what you prefer.

Investing in Your Sexual Relationship

Investing in your sexual relationship is important. It's important not because it's what you're supposed to do but because having good sex can be so fulfilling for both you and your partner. If you aren't already convinced, here are several more reasons why you should invest in your sexual relationship.

Marital Satisfaction

When your desire for sex is low, it may be easy to slip into feeling that sex isn't all that important to you or to your relationship's well-being. Yet research indicates that a good sex life may indeed be the key to marital satisfaction and stability, for both men and women. In one study, researchers studied 283 couples who had been married an average of thirty years. They found that couples who were satisfied with their sex lives tended to have higher levels of marriage quality. Because they had a strong sexual connection and felt satisfied and happy with their relationships, these couples also reported more stability in their marriages. These findings were equally true for both men and women and suggest that a good sex life causes relationship satisfaction (Yeh et al. 2006).

These results add to a large body of evidence that indicates how strongly sexual satisfaction is linked to marital quality (Young et al. 1998). And they're important to keep in mind, because they show that being sexually satisfied will help you feel more satisfied with your partner. And viewing your sex life as a way you can reconnect with your partner can potentially serve as a motivator for you to reinvest in your own sexuality. You can start to view sex as something that will contribute to your own satisfaction.

Sex as Stress Relief

A stressful day is usually associated with feeling burned-out and crabby. It's often a no-brainer that a busy, worry-filled day will leave you feeling anything but sexy. But what if at the end of a long, hard day, you viewed sex as something that could actually help you unwind and feel much better?

It turns out that for many people, having a stressful day leads to an increased likelihood of having sex the following day. Furthermore, those in happy relationships report that their sex lives serve as a source of stress relief (Ein-Dor and Hirschberger 2012). Sex can be a stress-reduction method because it stops the negative cycle of stress from building up, gaining momentum, and getting worse. Instead of having your stress escalate, you can begin to view having sex with your partner as a way to remove stress and refocus your energy.

Chemical Bonding

Without regular sex and touching, you don't have a chance for the "cuddle hormone" oxytocin to be released and work its magical bonding powers. Oxytocin, which is released during sex, is also released during cuddling and caressing. Hence oxytocin is known as the bonding chemical. Particularly when you're depressed, this mood-boosting chemical can be essential, both helping you bond with your partner and elevating your mood. Sex and touching also help you feel closer to your partner emotionally.

Developing Your Sexual Energy

You may think, *I am not a sexual person. I just don't have that much interest in sex.* However, you can suspend this belief or judgment about yourself and instead embrace the idea that sexuality is a natural, healthy part of being human.

Part of developing your sexual self is learning to notice feelings of discomfort about sex and exploring your sexual history. Having a sense of sexual identity means knowing what you're comfortable with, as well as what may be blocking your sexual energy, so that you can enjoy sex more. By allowing yourself to explore and integrate your sexual and sensual needs and desires, you can build a healthy sexual identity. Through experimentation with nongenital touching, caress, and foreplay, you can allow yourself to actively anticipate and participate in fulfilling sex.

Rather than just comply with obligatory, unenthusiastic sex for your partner's sake, you can make a conscious effort to rev up your own sexual appetite and invest in your sexual energy. Although sexual energy is an intangible—more a concept than something located in a particular place in your body—you may find it helpful to take a moment to imagine that you have within you a place that encompasses your sexual energy. Consider where your sexual energy resides—does it flow freely throughout your body? Is it difficult to locate? How comfortable are you with sharing this energy with your partner? When do you feel most in touch with this energy?

When you're having problems feeling in the mood, you can choose to focus your energy on this area of your life. It's about deciding that erotic feelings and sexual desire are one of the lifelines of your relationship and embracing the idea of becoming more in touch with your sexual side. It's about noticing the small moments throughout the day when your mind turns to sensual thoughts or when you find desire rising within. You can also create these moments intentionally, whether by reading a steamy novel, watching a sexy movie, or wearing an outfit out to dinner that makes you feel sexy. By taking the time to make room for sexuality in your daily life, you're increasing the flow of your erotic energy.

Sex therapists suggest increasing your sexual energy by taking it in small steps. These small steps slowly increase your sexual connection along with your sexual repertoire. In other words, you create a new relationship with sex through slowing down the process. By deconstructing the process and routine (or lack thereof) of what you imagine your sex life to be, you and your partner can grow and experience sexual energy in a new way.

The next section outlines several ideas for how to invest in your sexual relationship to reawaken your sexual energy.

Getting in the Mood

An encouraging fact about sex is that creating a willingness for sex and sexual touch leads to arousal and desire (Basson 2001). While the traditional model of sex holds that you must first have a desire for sex, which then turns into lustful action, it can just as easily (if not more) go the other way around. To assess your willingness for sex, ask yourself the following questions:

- How much time are you willing to invest in your sexual relationship?

- What other priorities could you reduce to make more time for sexual and sensual touch?

- What, if any, barriers come up for you in investing in your sexual relationship?

Even if you're not feeling in the mood, accepting the advances of your partner and getting started with the act of sex often bring about feelings of lust and desire. While you should never force yourself to have sex, there is a way in which you can bring a willingness to engage in sex with your partner, knowing that once you get going, those sexy, turned-on feelings will likely follow.

Making Time for Touch

The intense, smoldering chemistry that you feel with your partner in the initial phase of love usually lasts about six months to two years. Long-term sexual relationships require enthusiastic energy and attention. It's unrealistic to expect that the same level

143

of intensity can last a lifetime. Yet it's also a myth to believe that monogamous sex or sex as you age is bound to be unfulfilling, with passion remitting. Quite the contrary, sexuality can remain an integral and fulfilling aspect of your relationship into your eighties.

Part of fueling your sexual life is the act of making it a priority, and making time for touch, both sexual and sensual. While it may seem that sex should be spontaneous, the truth is that it can be just as sexy to plan ahead. Extended periods of time that are reserved for sex can be so important, like on weekends, where you may want to reserve one to two hours for the leisurely pleasure of intimate touching and sexual activities. On the other hand, having quickies can be good stress relief and can help maintain sexual activity during the workweek, when you may have less time for long encounters (Watson 2012).

The benefit of reserving a longer time for sexual experiences is that it allows time for pleasure to build. In her book *Wanting Sex Again*, Laurie Watson (2012) offers a 20/20 solution for women: twenty minutes of sexual foreplay and twenty minutes of sexual touch, for a total of forty minutes minimum in order to engender full desire and orgasm. While orgasm does not have to be the end goal of every sexual encounter, being able to achieve orgasm together can be an important part of fueling your sexual desire.

For Theresa, a major step in increasing her connection to her sexuality was recognizing that she's a slow boil, whereas he's an electric stove. She found that having her partner slowly, steadily massage her clitoris in a rhythmic manner while she lay against his chest on her back was the best way to allow her sexual energy to emerge. She experimented with touching herself in this manner during intercourse. This type of consistent, rhythmic touching is important for women's arousal and desire.

Theresa also found that making time to find out what types of touch and sexual acts Tom wanted helped her to access her own sexuality. Her own sexual energy expanded when she gave her partner pleasure and took the time to consider his needs.

Adding Flirtation

Another way to increase your sexual energy is by flirting more. Former clients of mine, Jeff and Anna, told me that their relationship started out with some major flirting going on. On each date, she would make an effort with her physical appearance and she would remark on how attractive Jeff looked. Jeff also made a special effort, bringing her on dates he thought she'd enjoy and giving her compliments. The energy they had during those early days was very flirtatious and led to even more chemistry and sexual energy. After they were married for a couple of years, however, their sexual energy diminished, and so did their flirtation.

I suggested that they reinstate date nights together. Their date night became a time to get dressed up for one another, share a glass of wine, giggle over an inside joke, and flirt with one another again. Having this time together made a world of difference in their sex life. Indeed, most couples notice that receiving compliments and attention from their partners, as well as responding with enthusiasm, increases sexual desire.

You can create romance by writing poetry, taking erotic photos, or by adding soft music and candlelight to the bedroom. You can slow dance, share a long glance at one another at parties, and make an effort to hold hands. You may want to introduce sex toys to expand your sexual repertoire and add variety that can keep you excited about your sexual encounters together. All of these can all be used to connect with your partner romantically and keep the air of flirtation alive.

Communicating About Sex

Being able to talk about sex, both inside and outside of the bedroom, is one predictor of good sexual functioning and satisfaction (Rehmen, Rellini, and Fallis 2011). Being open with your partner about your sexual preferences helps both of you get your needs met. It creates an atmosphere of intimacy, giving your partner access to your deepest desires. It shows trust and a level of vulnerability, which is so necessary for a close partnership.

Despite your desire to be open with your partner, it's fairly common to feel uncomfortable, initially, when discussing sex. No matter how long you've been together with someone, it can feel embarrassing or awkward to discuss your sex life. Yet getting past the initial discomfort is worth it. Discussing your sex life can often lead to relatively easy but very important changes that greatly help your physical relationship. It can even save your relationship.

Even if you're feeling discouraged about your sex life, it's important to convey a proactive, loving message to your partner. Avoid criticism. Instead, focus on explaining how important your sex life is to you and what you'd like to try to make it better. The key, when discussing anything regarding intimacy or sex with your partner, is to create a safe environment.

1. Pick a time outside of the bedroom—not before, during, or after sex—when both of you are free to discuss the topic.

2. Start out by letting your partner know why it's important to you to discuss your sex life and by sharing something about yourself. The goal is to communicate that you care about your partner and want to invest in your relationship. It's good to check in at this point to make sure that your partner is receptive and on board with the discussion. You should have discussions about sex and intimacy only when both of you are willing and feel it's a good time. You may say something like, "I know that I've been less interested in sex lately. I was hoping we could talk about a few things I've been thinking about that might help. Our relationship is really important to me, and I want to start spending more time on that part of it. How does that sound to you?"

3. If your partner is receptive, the next step is to give specific examples about what you'd like to try together. You can draw from the suggestions outlined earlier in this chapter,

such as sharing an intimate massage or taking a sensual shower together. You might also talk about some specific sexual desires or needs, such as trying out new positions or engaging in more foreplay.

4. End the conversation by scheduling some sensual time together. Be specific. For example, pick a Saturday afternoon when the kids are at their grandmother's house, and decide that noon to 2:00 p.m. will be couples time.

When you talk about your sex life, show that you're eager to know more about what your partner desires. She may like the idea of adding variety or new experiences to your sexual repertoire, such as mutual masturbation or foreplay before sex. Or maybe he would like to see more of a certain kind of sexual act happen more frequently, such as oral sex, manual stimulation, or using a certain position. The goal is to help balance your own sexual needs with your partner's.

Your discussion will likely lead you to consider how much sex you're having versus how much you'd like to be having. It can be helpful to ask direct questions. How often do you each want to have sex? Do you agree on this? Every couple needs to set their own standard for the right amount of sex, and it can cause major conflict when the two of you aren't on the same page. For some couples, having sex two times a week may feel like a perfect fit. Other couples may feel good with about twice a month. What matters is that both of you are comfortable with the regularity of your sex life. When you have differing expectations about frequency, and you are the partner with the lower desire for sex, it can be helpful to take your partner's needs into consideration.

Here are some questions to explore as you discuss your sexual style:

- *How do I initiate sex?*

- *How do I know when my partner is initiating sex?*

- *What's one of my favorite sexual positions? What's one of my partner's favorite positions?*

- *What do I wish we did more of in the bedroom?*

- *What types of touch feel best for me? What does my partner enjoy?*

- *What's one thing that we haven't tried together sexually that I'd like to do? What might my partner want to try?*

- *What sexual fantasies do I find arousing?*

- *How do I feel about the frequency of our sex life? Does it feel just the right amount, too little, or too much?*

- *What's my favorite part of my partner's body? What does my partner like best about me?*

- *When my partner touches me, am I able to enjoy the caress, or do I have concerns or worries that prevent me from staying in the moment?*

- *What's my favorite time of day for having sex? How about my partner?*

- *Do I like being more assertive or more passive during sex? Or do I prefer to go back and forth, taking turns on who takes the lead?*

- *Do I prefer the lights on or off during sex?*

- *What kind of new sexual acts or positions might I be curious or willing to explore?*

- *When do I have the best, most satisfying sex?*

These questions can serve as a basis for a conversation with your partner. You may want to review the list together, letting your partner know your answers and hearing your partner's responses as you go.

While it's crucial to talk about sex outside of the bedroom, it's also helpful to communicate what you like during sex. Give your spouse positive feedback about what you like in the moment, either by saying it or by giving nonverbal affirmations.

Making sounds and being free with your body can also help you to fully connect to your body and fully experience what's happening. The technique of exaggeration means that you immerse your whole body into your sexual activity (Barbach 2000). This means moving your body, making sounds, breathing deeply, and creating muscle tension. For both men and women, making sounds and touching your entire body during intercourse can help you feel more free and uninhibited, leading to better sexual experiences.

Conclusion

Understanding your sexual preferences is a lifelong process. You're desires, needs, and interests will fluctuate and change over time. Exploring the root cause of lowered sexual desire can be a gateway to learning how to reconnect to your sexual energy. What is exciting about taking the time to explore and expand your sexual awareness is that it can greatly contribute to your satisfaction, both sexually and emotionally, with your partner.

Remember that there is no perfect formula for having a good sexual relationship; instead, it's about being open to taking your time, exploring your bodies, sharing your needs, and being willing to consider your partner's needs. It's also about being flexible in the role you allow yourself to take.

The journey of sexual discovery within yourself can be deeply healing for you. Connecting with your partner sexually can also have a powerful, healing influence on your relationship. It's never too late to begin reconnecting with your sexual energy. Being in touch with your desires can be liberating and exciting, infusing your life with new energy and renewed passion.

chapter 7

Creating Intimate Understanding

Alice and Bryce have a strong relationship. Bryce feels lucky to have Alice in his life. "Alice means the world to me. She's my best friend. We get along so well. It's different from what I have with anyone else. Yes, she gets depressed sometimes, and it's hard, but it's part of the package. We've learned to get through it." When Alice talks to me about Bryce, it's clear she values him. "Bryce is amazing. He is so patient, caring, and loving. I'm very lucky to have him," she says. Alice has struggled with depression on and off for several years, but their relationship has remained strong. What allows Bryce to understand where Alice is coming from, even though he doesn't experience depression himself?

It's not that Alice and Bryce have a perfect life. They have bad days and they argue, just like other couples. But they've learned that they can trust one another with their feelings. The deepest component of their connection is that they feel supported and cared for by one another. Both Alice and Bryce have learned the value of feeling understood.

This chapter focuses on helping you find ways to understand and be understood in your relationship. You'll identify new ways to nourish what most matters in your relationship: sharing and validating each other, growing through conflict, and increasing your intimacy. You'll learn some new communication tool, as well as ways to validate each other's experience, accept differing points of view, and empathize with your partner even when you see things differently. You'll identify the stages of conflict you may encounter and explore how to handle conflict in a way that helps you bond with your partner.

Successful relationships happen when partners support each other in times of need and make themselves emotionally available for each other (Skowron 2000). This chapter will help you move from feeling misunderstood and alone to being part of a team.

Sharing and Validation

Intimacy comes down to two key words: sharing and validating. If you can share how you're feeling and receive validation, you will have intimacy. Your relationship will be most successful when you're able to share your inner world with your partner—your real thoughts, feelings, and desires—and when your partner, in turn, is able to really hear you. Similarly, your partner needs to be able to share his or her inner world with you, and feel understood by you (Cutrona 2007). When you use a validating style of interaction, you build trust and intimacy (Fruzzetti and Iverson 2004). You create an enduring bond.

The Power of Validation

Recollect a moment when you felt really understood. Perhaps you remember a caring teacher in grade school who seemed to know exactly what to say when you were upset. Maybe you can think of a friend who dropped everything when you called with exciting news and was eager to share your joy. Remember the last time you felt really heard, understood, and listened to. It's a powerful feeling, isn't it?

Validation in your relationship means that when your partner tells you about her day or shares her feelings, you stay with her in the moment, honoring that experience. You join her world and see things from her point of view. It's a way of showing you understand and accept your partner's thoughts and feelings, just as they are. If your partner is upset about something, validating those feelings will help him feel less upset and less vulnerable, whereas invalidating behaviors do the opposite; they make your partner feel misunderstood, dismissed, and alone.

Because the symptoms of depression may cause you to ruminate and focus more on yourself, it's critical that you learn the skills of validation to help your partner feel connected and understood by you, even when you're depressed. Much the same way, when you're partner learns to validate your experiences, even if she doesn't share them, it creates understanding. Overall, it will help most if both of you learn these skills.

Providing Validation

While the concept of validation may seem simple, it can sometimes be a little tricky to execute. Imagine your partner coming home and telling you he is furious because he found out he needs to work over the holiday weekend. What is your first reaction? You might feel protective of your spouse, or upset at the situation, and have the natural urge to try to fix the problem. You might offer him advice on how to solve it. While intuitively it may seem helpful to give suggestions, it can be invalidating to your partner. He may not be looking for help in the form of a solution; he probably has already tried to find ways to solve the problem. He might feel even more frustrated in hearing advice, no matter how good your intention.

So how do you effectively listen to and validate your partner? Here are six key components to help guide your conversations.

Mindful listening. The first component of validation is mindful listening (Fruzzetti and Iverson 2004). Mindful listening occurs when you pay attention to what your partner is saying while momentarily suspending your own judgments and reactions. You temporarily let go of the need to advise, change, help, or fix the situation. Your put your own thoughts on the back burner; your focus, instead, is on your partner's current experience. You can show that you're listening by stopping whatever you are doing and giving your undivided attention. The process of being fully listened to is, in itself, validating for your partner.

Acknowledgment and acceptance. The next step is to acknowledge what your partner has said, or what you believe he is feeling, based on his words. You might say, in response to the news about having to work over the weekend, "I can see you're upset," or "You seem discouraged." Rather than trying to cheer your partner up, you accept how he's feeling, allowing him space to be upset. It is validating for your partner to know that you accurately acknowledge and accept his emotions.

Validating does not equal agreeing. You can accept your partner's feelings even if you don't agree with him. For instance, imagine that your partner is feeling hopeless about his parenting abilities. She feels overwhelmed and thinks he doesn't do well with the kids, while you see that he's a good dad and you know how much the kids adore him. If he brings up how he feels discouraged, you might validate his point of view by saying, "I feel really lost and incompetent with the kids sometimes too. I know how it feels to be discouraged. I see what an amazing job you do, and I don't think that you're doing a bad job. But I know it doesn't always feel that way in the moment." In this example, you're acknowledging your partner's feelings without necessarily agreeing or sharing the same sentiment.

Ask questions. If your partner presents a difficult problem or situation, validate that it's an important topic by finding out more about what's going on. Find out more about how your partner is feeling or what the problem is by asking open-ended questions.

- "How did it happen?"

- "What was most upsetting?"

- "What was your reaction to that?"

- "How are you feeling about things now?"

- "What do you wish would happen?"

When you gently ask questions to clarify the experience, it can be very gratifying for your partner. It shows you are giving weight to his concerns, and it shows you care and want to really listen.

Be emotionally available. Allowing yourself to be affected by your partner's words, actions, and feelings is a vital component of being emotionally available. Your partner's ability to affect you shows that you're open emotionally, that you're receptive to your partner's ideas and feelings. It's important to share that you're affected. "It hurts me to see you struggle." Or "It really makes me reconsider my stance on this issue when I hear you explain it that way." Being influenced by your partner validates her sense that what she says matters to you (Gottman and Silver 1999).

Show you understand. Use validating statements, such as "I would feel that way too," or "It makes sense to me that you'd feel that way, given the circumstances," to let your partner know you see why he might feel the way he does (Schröder-Abé and Schütz 2011). You can also use nonverbal communication, such as giving him a hug if he feels lonely, making him a cup of tea if he feels jittery, or giving him space if he needs time to think.

It's also important to recognize that you are different people who sometimes have different needs. For example, if you were in your partner's shoes, you might prefer to talk over a glass of wine, or you might prefer cuddling and holding one another while talking. It's easy to assume that your partner would want the same thing. But your partner may have a different idea of what is validating in the moment. To discover your partner's needs, ask what would be most helpful:

- "Would it be helpful for you to hear my opinion?"

- "Should we brainstorm some ideas to help solve this?"

- "Are you tired of talking about this and want to do something to get your mind off of it?"

Validation works best when you're willing to give comfort in ways that work best for your partner and your partner is willing to give you validation in ways that work best for you.

Validation Timing

Sometimes it's easier to be there for your partner when times are good. Celebrating good moments together comes naturally. But when your partner needs your validation the most are the difficult moments in life. Just as feelings of loss, rejection, or changes to your identity can be triggers for your depression, your partner is more likely to need your support and empathy during difficult times, like when he or she is experiencing

- Loss, such as the death of a family member or close friend

- Rejection, such as having a difficult encounter with a family member who is critical of her

- Shift in job status, such as missing a promotion, losing a job, or taking a new position

- Stressful periods related to conflicting work, home, and personal needs

- Transitions, like when having a child leave for college or when entering into retirement

Changes in your partner's mood or behavior may signal that he is having trouble coping, even if there is no obvious change at work or at home. This is a good time to show empathy as well.

Keep in mind that these times likely affect you too. If your partner loses her job, for instance, it's natural to think about how it affects you: *I have to work more hours. I have to pay the bills. I have to cope with this.* It's important to take care of yourself while not becoming too caught up in your own reaction. Take time to ask yourself if you're paying attention to your partner's needs in a validating, thoughtful way: *Yes, this affects my workload and places more strain on me. But how must she be feeling right now? Perhaps she feels she's placing a burden on me, or she's really being hard on herself.* While it's not always easy, being able to focus on how your partner feels can actually help you avoid getting lost in your own concerns.

Barriers to Validation

You may have a difficult time with giving or receiving validation. If, when growing up, you were taught to suck it up, be strong, and move on, then validation can seem overly sensitive. If you didn't receive validation from your parents, it might feel weak to think you need to be understood emotionally. Giving and receiving validation can be an almost intimidating or off-putting process, particularly for males, who are often socialized to see being emotional as a weakness.

If you experience some discomfort with the idea of validation, I encourage you to be open to trying it out. See what happens if you allow your partner to validate you. Validate your partner the next time he needs you, and notice how it affects your relationship. You will probably see that you feel more connected, you argue less, and you resolve problems together in a more productive manner.

If you continue to feel uncomfortable with validation, you may want to talk to a therapist, who can help you introduce validation into your relationship. You can do this without losing your sense of self and independence. The key is to be true to who you are while also considering what your partner is thinking, feeling, and needing.

Similarly, giving and receiving validation may be a difficult concept for your partner to embrace. Again, this may go back to old messages that your partner received as a child, causing her to feel that it's not safe, wise, or necessary to confide in others. People with avoidant attachment styles may have particular trouble with validation, since connecting with emotion often poses a threat to the structure of interactions they are comfortable using.

Moving past the barriers to interacting with your partner in a validating way takes practice. If you're not used to communicating this way, it may be hard to know when and how to do it. The next exercise will help you practice accurate listening and empathy.

Exercise: Practicing Validation

Read the sample scripts. Then create your own script to learn how to effectively validate and affirm your partner.

1. Cue: Your partner's body language is tense: his arms are crossed and eyes are downcast.

    Nonvalidating response: (harsh tone) "What's wrong with you? You look miserable."

    Validating response: (curious, soft tone) "You seem tense. Anything I can do?"

2. Cue: Your partner has tears in her eyes or is crying.

    Nonvalidating response: (impatient tone) "You're so emotional. It's not that bad; you'll be fine."

    Validating response: (warm, concerned tone) "I'm sorry you're upset. I wish I could make it better."

3. Cue: Your partner says, "I'm lonely."

    Nonvalidating response: (dismissive, critical tone) "What's there to be lonely about? I'm right here. You have plenty of friends."

    Validating response: (open, receptive tone) "I'm so sorry to hear you're feeling lonely. I wouldn't have guessed you're lonely. It seems like you have lots of people in your life, including me. I'm always here for you. Tell me what's going on."

4. Cue: Your partner tells you he wants to talk about something important.

    Nonvalidating response: (dismissive, annoyed tone) "I've had a really long day. Can it wait?"

Validating response: (accepting, cooperative tone) "Give me just one second to finish this email. I want to give you my full attention."

Now it's your turn. Think about some cues your partner has given you in the past and some different responses that you could give. Write down examples of both invalidating and validating responses. Use this format to complete the exercise:

1. Cue from your partner:

2. Nonvalidating response:

3. Nonvaliding tone of voice:

4. Validating response you can give instead:

5. Validating tone of voice:

Note that, in addition to what you say, your body language and tone of voice can make the difference between an invalidating and a validating response.

Now, think of some times when you are the one who has needed validation. Think about the cues you may use to let your partner know that you need support. What responses from your partner do you find the most validating? What do you find the least validating? Write down what you've learned and share it with your partner.

You can let your partner know you're working on this skill. It may be helpful to ask your partner to tell you when she needs validation and to remind you gently in the moment if she would prefer a different response from what you've given.

The Importance of Sharing

As much as validating is a crucial element of intimacy, it's only half of the equation (Fruzzetti and Iverson 2004). The other half is sharing how you're feeling with your partner. Without sharing, validation can't occur.

When miscommunication or lack of clear communication causes you to feel hurt, ignored, minimized, or distant from your partner, it can be a roadblock in your relationship. The reality is that your partner may not always fully understand you. Your partner can't know how you feel. It's important to say what's going on inside.

It's often lonely when you feel misunderstood. To make sure your partner has the chance to really understand you, it's important to communicate as accurately as possible.

Look Within

The first step in accurate sharing is to look within before you say anything. While it can be helpful to talk out your feelings to discover how you feel about something (extroverts, in particular, tend to prefer this method of sharing), there are times when it can be helpful to take time to reflect before talking with your partner. In these instances, give yourself space to ponder what's happening. Journaling may help you to sort out your thoughts. To facilitate the process, answer these questions:

- What's the trigger situation (what caused this)?

- How do you feel about it and why?

- What are some possible solutions?

- From whom can you get support to make these solutions work?

After looking within, you will be in a better position to share your feelings with your partner.

Be Willing to Be Vulnerable

Sharing your joys and sorrows with your partner can make you feel vulnerable. But exposing some vulnerability—showing your partner that you have a weakness or that you need him or that you are confused—is an essential part of really knowing each other. Sharing makes you more accessible because it shows your partner what's really in your heart. While it may be outside of your comfort zone, sharing allows you to receive support that you couldn't otherwise get if you remained closed off. Exposing your feelings also encourages your partner to share with you, as it sets the stage for a more open relationship.

Avoid Blame

Sharing your thoughts, feelings, wishes, or needs should not come at the expense of your partner. Blaming your partner will push the two of you apart and cause your partner to resist hearing you out. An example of this might be saying, "I'm feeling really disappointed in how you're acting." If how you're feeling relates directly to your partner, try to focus on the situation and express how you feel rather than blame your partner for something he did or didn't do. Elicit him as a partner in solving the problem you both have. And be sure to take ownership of your part in the matter.

For example, Madison had become irritable because her husband had been working long hours lately and hadn't been able to help with household tasks as much as before. If she were to share her feelings in an accusatory tone—"I've been so irritable because you're never home and it's really upsetting me"—he might become defensive and be unreceptive. Instead, to avoid sounding overly critical and harsh toward her husband, she said, "I know I've been crabby lately, and I'm sorry. I want you to know I feel bad about being mean. I think I've been upset that you're home less and feel like I'm picking up the slack. Is there a way we can work on making this better?" In this way, she shared her concern and also took ownership for her role in the situation.

Aim to Share, Not Vent

Especially if you're dealing with depression, it's important to share where you are emotionally without getting stuck in a pattern that causes you to feel more negatively. Venting, rather than sharing, is not healthy for either you or your partner. When you say, "I feel miserable and hopeless about our relationship. I hate my job and it's not getting better. Nothing makes it better, and I really need you to validate how badly I'm feeling," you may intend for your words to be cathartic, but this kind of venting is actually toxic for both of you when it becomes a common pattern. It's likely to make you feel more depressed, and your partner will quickly lose her ability to feel empathy for you.

Instead, focus on sharing how you're feeling with an emphasis on checking in, letting your partner know when you're having a hard time, and thinking about how you can move forward: "I'm in a place where everything feels miserable! I know it's not true, but I can't help but feel discouraged. So if I seem upset, that's why." In this case, you're telling your partner what's going on inside of you. You're not criticizing your partner or ruminating on your painful feelings.

When sharing is in danger of becoming venting, it's helpful to employ other coping methods you've learned, such as self-soothing, mindful awareness of emotions, practicing gratitude and acceptance, or deep breathing. Slowing down can help decrease the intensity of your emotions. If you're unable to talk things through in that moment, it will help your partner if you can explain what's going on inside. Letting your partner know that you need some space or want to work it out for yourself is being considerate of his thoughts and feelings.

Requesting Validation

It's okay to ask your partner for what you need, or clue her into how she can help. Using the skills of validation you've learned, think about which forms of validation will be most helpful to you and then share them with your partner.

- "I really need a hug right now."

- "I've already thought of a million solutions to this problem, but I just want to tell you about how frustrated I am. It would be great if you're willing to listen and just be here for me."

- "Have you ever been through something like this? I'd love to feel like you can relate to what I'm going through."

- "I'm feeling stuck right now. What do you think we should do?"

When you believe your partner will respond well, you will be more comfortable sharing your concerns and feelings.

Growing Through Conflict

One of the ideas that this book has tried to impart is that your relationship will have troubles at times, and every couple will experience conflict. What defines a good relationship is not lack of conflict but how you handle your conflict when it arrives.

This section will help you make up and forgive in a loving way, learn how to identify your core conflicts and solve problems with your partner, and set relationship goals that will help you define your relationship as your home base. With a secure base, you'll be better able to withstand the aftermath of a painful argument.

After a Fight

Sometimes emotions get out of hand, tension builds, and *boom*—a fight explodes between the two of you. Both of you said things you didn't mean, tossing out a few below-the-belt comments, and at the time, it seemed that all was fair in love and war. All your good intentions about validating and sharing went out the door. Today, however, in the cold, harsh light of day and with a cooler head, things seem like a mess. How do you begin to repair the damage of a bad argument?

The key is to reach out to try to make it better. All couples fight—what's important is finding ways to make you both feel safe and loved again.

Making Up

When you and your partner have a fight, what helps you move past the argument? Think back to the last conflict you had—how did it get resolved? Who between the two of you usually reaches out to make up? Do you tend to be the person who usually apologizes, or is your partner the one who tends to make the first move?

Relationships that are healthy grow through conflict when partners are able to reach out to each other to make things better and forgive one another (Bradbury and Fincham 1990). The aim should be to share this role fifty-fifty, where both of you look to come together to soothe each other's hurt feelings, meeting each other halfway. The overarching goal in making up is to reiterate that you care for your partner and to help him feel safe again.

Goodwill Gestures

One of you has to make the first move in making up after an argument. Perhaps there's a certain bashful, playful face your partner makes that signals "Aw shucks, I'm sorry," or a key phrase you use to signal that you're ready to move on, such as "I want us to be on good terms again." These are goodwill gestures. Using humor or an inside joke can serve as a goodwill gesture to help you get past an argument; moving from an angry or irritated tone of voice to a softer, gentler tone of voice is also a goodwill gesture. Goodwill gestures can come in the form of backing down by admitting you were wrong, even if you still think you have a good point, because it's for the greater good. They can come in the form of validating your partner or agreeing to disagree while reiterating that you love your partner in spite of your differences.

When your partner makes a goodwill gesture, it's important to be receptive. If she writes you a note with the words, "I'm sorry :)," tell her you don't like fighting, either. Acknowledge that she's making an effort, and learn to accept her goodwill gesture for the sake of your relationship.

If Apologies Are Hard

Reaching out to your partner after an argument may be hard for you. Sometimes it's difficult to set aside your pride and admit that you hurt the other person. Other times, it feels unfair—perhaps you didn't mean to hurt your partner's feelings. The key here is being aware that your intention toward your partner may be different from your effect on him. For instance, Scott signed up for a softball league that plays on Saturday mornings. When his wife learned about this, she became very upset: "Saturday mornings are when we have our family breakfasts and take a walk together. That's a really special time for me. I thought it was for you too." Scott hadn't intended to hurt his wife's feelings by scheduling something during family time, but the effect of his actions had been hurtful. In this case, it's easy to differentiate intention from effect. If the effect is hurting your partner—even if you didn't intend to hurt her—then it's important to acknowledge how her feelings were affected and work to make amends.

You may hold back from going to your partner because, deep down, you fear that apologizing or reaching out will signal weakness. Seeing yourself as weak may make you feel vulnerable or cause you to worry that your partner will use your weakness against you to shame or humiliate you. If this is the case, talk to your partner about why it's hard for you to admit any wrongdoing. Explain that you worry your apology will be used as a weapon to make you feel bad. Sharing this will likely soften your partner's response. Work with your partner to make sure that your words are received in an accepting way.

If You Apologize Too Much

Think back to the past few months of your relationship. Does it ever feel like you do a whole lot of soothing and appeasing of your partner, but he never seems to apologize for anything? You may be accepting too much responsibility in your relationship and may be missing the soothing and comfort that you need. Since it's pretty unlikely that you are solely to blame in every disagreement, it's time to think about why this might be happening. Perhaps you played the role of peacemaker in your family of origin. Perhaps conflict makes you so uncomfortable that you'll go to any lengths to avoid it. If this is the case, it may be helpful to challenge yourself to allow your partner to come to you. Let your partner know when you need to be soothed and comforted.

Identifying Your Conflict

In the heat of an argument, thoughts tend to be irrational and emotions tend to rule, and it's hard to solve anything. Instead, approaching your conflict when both of you are calm can work wonders. I call this "striking while the iron is cold." In order to do this, make sure you're thinking about the conflict in a time of peace and calm, as opposed to in the middle of the problem or right before an issue needs to be resolved. For instance, rather than argue with each other about whether your son can borrow the car—or have the argument erupt when he asks you for it—talk over the question beforehand, so you have a clear plan.

When you have a conflict, the first step toward resolving it is to clearly identify the core problem and look at how it's affecting your relationship. To identify the core problem, write down your primary concerns, describing what you think the problem is. This exercise will help you to clarify what's bothering you.

Exercise: Clarifying Your Conflict

Think of a core conflict in your relationship. Use the following questions to give you clarity about this conflict:

- What is the primary issue, or concern, as you see it?

- What are your expectations related to this conflict?

- Which of your values come into play related to this conflict?

- What do you think are your partner's expectations or values regarding the issue?

- How is this conflict affecting your relationship?

Doing this exercise (and asking your partner to do the same if he or she desires) will help to clarify what is really going on.

Once you've identified and defined the particular issue that you'd like to resolve, you can come up with some potential solutions. This works best when you can brainstorm with your partner.

Brainstorming Together

Active brainstorming occurs when two partners are both openly aware of a core conflict and engaged in trying to make changes. Even if previous efforts have been unsuccessful or ineffective, the key is that both of you are open to continuing to brainstorm for ways to approach the conflict.

Your goal should be to approach the problem in a new way, looking for solutions to the problem while also keeping in mind your larger goals. You can take these steps to resolve your conflict, as Lily and Hansen did to resolve their conflict and tension over having differing political views.

1. Clarify your wishes and goals related to resolving the issue. Ask yourself, what would be better in your relationship if this conflict between you were resolved?

   Hansen: There'd be less arguing.

   Lily: If we didn't fight so much about politics, our relationship would be less strained, and I'd feel more respected.

2. What might you be doing differently if the conflict were resolved? For this question, imagine that the conflict you've

had is no longer a source of conflict. What would be different? How would you be acting differently, and how would it affect your life?

Hansen: I'd be less stubborn. It might make Lily happier, which makes me happy.

Lily: If this weren't a source of conflict, then we'd be able to discuss our views without getting into a fight. I'd be acting differently by being able to hear his opinions without judging or feeling hurt. I would try to learn acceptance for his views when they differ from my own.

3. What might your partner be doing differently if the problem were solved? Again, imagine that the conflict were already resolved. How might your partner be acting differently?

Hansen: She'd be more open minded, hear me out.

Lily: He would be acting differently by respecting my opinions and not criticizing the views I hold.

4. In what ways has this conflict hurt your relationship? Describe the ways that this conflict has interfered with your life, whether it's increased your fighting, caused you to lose trust, made your feel more insecure, or is placing extra strain on your sex life.

Hansen: It creates tension at family gatherings sometimes. Lily gets upset if we argue around her folks.

Lily: It makes it difficult to decide how to spend money if one of us wants to donate to a cause, and it creates hostility between the two of us.

5. What is your pattern of interaction around this conflict? Notice if there is a demand/withdraw interaction when the problem

arises between you. Do one or both of you tend to become combative and angry, or silent and cold?

Hansen: Lily gets tired of arguing and usually ends the conversation first.

Lily: We both tend to become heated, and then we both withdraw from each other.

6. Have you had similar problems in the past? How did you handle those problems? Were those interventions successful? What worked well with those solutions, and what didn't work well?

Hansen: We usually listen to each other pretty well and agree on most things.

Lily: We have somewhat different religious views, and we've found a way to accept each other's point of view. When we were buying a house, we wanted different features in the house. We ended up making a list of what we wanted and then we compromised.

7. What are some possible outcomes or solutions to your current problem? Include every idea that the two of you can come up with, regardless of whether it seems like a viable option. It's okay to include "agree to disagree" as an outcome. In this case, agreeing to disagree might mean the two of you negotiate what you're willing to do to compromise or you talk about how you can continue to have a strong relationship despite the conflict not being fully resolved.

Lily and Hansen's list:

"We could never talk about politics again."

"When politics comes up, we both will work on validating how the other sees the situation while maintaining our own perspectives."

"When either of us becomes upset about the topic, we'll agree to take a break from the discussion."

"We can try to learn from the other's point of view and try to be more open to why each of us feels how we feel."

Rather than trying to find a solution right away, brainstorming helps you understand what could make things better and how your relationship will benefit from finding a solution. The next step is to set your goals.

Setting Relationship Goals

You can set new goals for your relationship with the information you gain in brainstorming resolutions to core conflicts. Relationship goals are just like any other goals you'd set in life, such as working on making it to the gym more often or cutting back on your weekend workload, in that setting goals helps you create a vision and a clear way to make that vision happen. It also fosters a sense of teamwork and cooperation. Look at the essence of what gets lost through your conflicts, and work to strengthen that part of your relationship.

Exercise: Setting Relationship Goals

Take the following steps to make a more secure foundation for your relationship:

1. State your goal as an outcome. What is the outcome you are looking to achieve? In other words, what will be different in your relationship if you reach your goal?

    Example: "My goal is to interact with my partner in a loving and validating manner, even when we may disagree."

2. State specific actions that will facilitate the goal. You may want to focus on the skills you've learned in this book and make a commitment to use specific skills. When you state specific actions, focus on

what you will contribute to the goal rather than what your partner needs to do.

Example: "Specifically, I will work to validate her when I notice she's upset about this issue. I will work to share with her how I'm feeling rather than let resentment build up. I will work on keeping my tone of voice calm and respectful, and I will take a twenty-minute break if I find I'm escalating into destructive anger."

3. Measure progress toward the goal. How will you know if your goals are being achieved?

    Example: "I've noticed we haven't had any angry blowups, and I think we've both been more forgiving toward one another. I know our goals are working when we're getting along better."

Having relationship goals helps you stay connected to what really matters to you in your relationship.

Increasing Your Intimacy

Much of the discussion in this book has centered on how you can turn around the effects of depression by fostering intimacy. Developing and enriching closeness is one of the best parts of being in a relationship; closeness is the reward that comes from making it through the rough patches. This section reviews some of the best ways to maintain your bond.

Make Time to Bond

When you live together or have a family together, you share daily tasks with your partner. It's important to remember that these daily routines are just one aspect of your relationship rather than its sole purpose. If most of your time is spent divvying up tasks and taking care of business, the relationship will suffer. You need to take time to have fun, to connect emotionally, and to have positive discussions with your partner, and you need to keep this time separate from reviewing household tasks or resolving conflicts. Take time for quality bonding.

The purpose of this time together is to develop a shared life that is full of meaning and possibilities. Perhaps you want to discuss philosophy together or contemplate the meaning of life. Or you can spend this time exploring ideas for your next vacation. When it's date time, try to turn off the decision-making mode and allow yourself to relax and enjoy being with your partner. Make an effort to visit places you want to go together. Chat over coffee or a glass of wine while you watch the sunset. Share with your partner how much you love her, what you treasure about her, and how much she means to you. You can never say it too much.

Plan Special Times Together

Recall the last time you were really excited about an upcoming event or occasion. The anticipation was half the fun. When you create an expectation of having a good time with your significant other, the relationship benefits from the boost to your mood, so make sure you plan times for doing something exciting together or for taking a relaxing weekend away from all your shared responsibilities.

"What if my spouse and I have nothing in common anymore?" you may wonder. The goal is to create a shared life through planning and weaving your lives together. Rather than wait for it to occur naturally, you can find ways to create shared experiences.

After learning of this idea, my clients Yolanda and Tim decided to plan a white-water rafting expedition. They stretched out the planning phase, taking a few drives up to the river, going on picnics, and taking a few short, easy trips with guides. They studied maps of the area and learned which materials to pack for camping. Tim and Yolanda felt really close to each other as they were preparing for this adventure and anticipating the rewards. Tim felt invigorated by the change in scenery, and Yolanda loved the challenge. They ended up making more time for one another and bonding over their adventures.

Another couple, Ming and Sandi decided get back into photography, a hobby they both had enjoyed in college. Sandi loved finding new places to photograph, and Ming liked comparing their shots, learning from Sandi's perspective and approach. They both looked forward to there photo-taking trips together. Ming printed out some of his favorite photos and Sandi framed them. The photos reminded the two of their good times together, and represented more fun times to come.

Add Novelty

Surprise and innovation keep your relationship fresh. Emily surprised her boyfriend with tickets to a ball game. Jesse surprised his wife by planning a picnic and taking her to the park one Sunday afternoon. When your partner surprises you, you feel an extra rush of excitement. Similarly, offering your partner a gift, a nice meal, or a loving card feels even more wonderful when it's not on a holiday and is an unexpected delight.

Create Daily Rituals

While surprise and novelty foster intimacy, it's also good to have regular activities that you look forward to doing together. Daily rituals together don't have to be grand or intricate gestures. In fact, creating a few simple, easy rituals is all you need to reap the benefits of connection. Here are some suggestions.

Separation and Reunion Ritual

One couple I work with, Anika and Dev, leave for work every morning with a kiss goodbye. When Dev returns home from work, he greets her with a hug and kiss. When they go to bed, each and every night they both say, "Goodnight, I love you," and seal it with a kiss. Dev and Anika maintain these rituals, without fail. The separation and reunion kisses are meaningful to Dev, giving him a chance to connect with her. This ritual makes Anika feel loved, and she would miss it if she didn't get her daily dose of affection when saying hello, goodbye, and goodnight.

You too can create a daily greeting and farewell ritual with your partner to help you connect through transitions. Having a ritual and being mindful of one another's presence is a powerful way to connect.

Another powerful ritual is having a regular evening check-in before bedtime. You may take some time before bed just to snuggle up and talk to each other. The time spent together at bedtime can become a treasured practice.

Daily Meal Ritual

Eating meals together is another strong tradition, allowing you time to talk and connect each day. Having nightly meals together is a routine that can be tough to keep every night, especially if you have conflicting schedules and activities, but making this a priority will benefit your relationship. You can set a goal to sit down and eat together at least six meals a week. This may mean meeting for lunch on your midday break when dinner won't work that day. Imagine leaving the office once a week to meet up with your loved one at the nearby corner café. It can be a fun break in your day. For my clients Trey and Zoe, this means meeting every Friday for lunch because Trey works late on Fridays. They both look forward to their Friday lunch each week.

If you miss having a meal together, you can sit down with each other when your partner arrives home in the evening. This way you can maintain your ritual of coming together.

Touch Base During Your Day

Another couple, Tamara and Xavier, make a ritual of touching base during their workday, usually at least twice a day. Usually Tamara will email Xavier, telling him a funny story she overheard on the way to work or sharing an interesting article she read. Xavier always returns her messages and includes some details about his day or asks about their plans for the evenings. Despite his busy schedule, he looks forward to hearing from Tamara. Both treasure their daily check-ins and feel there's a void if they don't hear from one another. Whether it's a phone call at lunchtime each day or an email or text exchange, the ritual of touching base during your workday keeps you tuned in.

Use Endearing Nicknames

Calling each other by playful nicknames can be something you do daily. Whether you use the same nicknames all the time or change them occasionally, the sentiment is there. Having nicknames for each other solidifies your special affection for one another.

Create Weekly Rituals

Weekly rituals also create the anticipation of fun and connection together. What better way to get through a long workweek than to know you'll be having a relaxing brunch on Saturday, just the two of you? Maybe it's doing the Sunday crossword puzzle together each weekend or getting dressed up and going out for a date one night each week. Perhaps you have a favorite show you watch together on Thursday evenings, cuddled up on the couch together after putting the kids to bed. The purpose is to have a set time or space where you know you'll have time together to look forward to and reconnect.

Foster Equality and Acceptance

Treating each other as equals and holding mutual respect for one another is a cornerstone of intimacy. After all, intimacy is about trusting your partner, seeking comfort and a safe haven in one another. Knowing that your partner respects you gives you a sense of security, an assurance that your partner accepts you for who you are. Similarly, it's vital that you accept his essence and respect his core self. In order to have acceptance for each other, there has to be a sense of respect as well as room for individuality. You accept that part of what makes your partner unique and wonderful is her flaws, idiosyncrasies, and foibles. Accepting that your partner will have imperfections, or behaviors that annoy you, allows you to let go of the smaller concerns that could otherwise bog down your relationship. If the worst thing your partner does is forget to put down the toilet seat or fold his clothes, you can learn to accept and live with these traits, no problem, if it will make for a stronger and more satisfying relationship.

We feel most connected to those who we feel really know us in life. While recognizing that you can never fully understand your partner's experience, it's crucial that you make an effort to know your partner as well as you can. What are her fears? What makes him feel exhilarated? Showing you care through active listening and validation is what ultimately contributes to your partner feeling understood.

Working through conflict and having larger relationship goals help you to keep things in perspective. Awareness of your own thoughts, sensations, and feelings, while being mindful of your partner's moods and needs, allows understanding to flow through your relationship.

Conclusion

When you make your relationship a high priority in your life, the rewards are clear. Spending more time together doing things you care about, setting relationship goals, taking the time to listen to each other—these are the moments that define and strengthen what the two of you have, helping stave off depression and despair. And when fights or disagreements occur, you know that there are always ways to recover and make things better again. The important part is noticing the ruptures and giving your relationship the attention it needs.

Final Thoughts

Sometimes, the most powerful way to approach your depression is to recognize what a large effect you can have on your own relationship. Depression makes you feel helpless, but you know differently now. Being mindful of your emotions helps you manage your painful feelings and allows you to connect to positive emotions. Being in the present moment, feeling gratitude for your partner, and learning to validate your partner are powerful tools for connection. Learning to work through your own emotions while being mindful of your partner's experience gives you new options to respond more effectively to your partner. The patterns of demand/withdraw are quieted, paving the way for loving-kindness.

Looking inward, whether at your sexual energy and sensuality or at your life values and goals, expands your self-awareness. Through self-awareness, you develop greater attunement to the needs of your partner, and the ability to tune into your own.

Asking for your needs to be met is a brave choice. Such asking requires vulnerability and sharing, as well as introspection and the ability to listen to yourself. It also challenges you to ask yourself, *What am I really yearning for?* Rather than retreat or withdraw into depression, you remain present with yourself and with partner.

Having true intimacy with your partner means that you have inner strengths and assets to draw on in times of need. You're able to manage your painful feelings; you're able to be mindful of the temptation to withdraw or criticize. And, instead of giving in to that impulse, you're able to focus on looking within and riding out the waves of emotion. Your actions are directed toward using behaviors that add to intimacy, even when depression tries to pull you in a destructive direction. Depression will attempt to thwart your love: it may lead you to lash out or shift difficult emotions onto your partner; it may try to tell you that you can never feel better; it may try to get you to withdraw and push your partner away when you most need him or her. To counter it, you can use your strengths to guide you: your values, your passions, your commitment, and your ability to empathize with your partner and have compassion for yourself as you make it through the toughest moments in life.

This book has taught you skills to help you stay connected, despite depression's presence. Achieving lasting intimacy can indeed be a reality for you.

I encourage you to take those moments of insight you've gained and use them to collaborate with your partner. Fighting the uninvited guest of depression ultimately works best as a team effort. Applying the skills and techniques that matter most to you and your partner will help you make lasting changes for the better.

Long after you've finished reading these pages, please carry with you the message that depression does not have to define, destroy, or devalue your relationship. With your relationship bond flourishing with passion, tenderness, and understanding, depression doesn't stand a chance.

References

Ainsworth, M. D. S., M. C. Blehar, E. Walters, and S. Wall. 1978. *Patterns of Attachment: A Psychological Study of the Strange Situation.* Hillsdale, NJ: Lawrence Erlbaum Associates.

American Psychiatric Association. 2013. *Diagnostic and Statistical Manual of Mental Disorders (DSM-V)*, 5th ed. Washington, DC: American Psychiatric Association.

Barbach, L. 2000. *For Yourself: The Fulfillment of Female Sexuality.* New York: Penguin Putnam.

Basson, R. J. 2001. "Using a Different Model for Female Sexual Response to Address Women's Problematic Low Sexual Desire." *Journal of Sex and Marital Therapy* 27 (5): 395–403.

Baucom, B. R., P. T. McFarland, and A. Christensen. 2010. "Gender, Topic, and Time in Observed Demand/Withdraw Interaction in Cross- and Same-Sex Couples." *Journal of Family Psychology* 24 (3): 233–42.

Beardslee, W. R., T. R. G. Gladstone, and E. E. O'Connor. 2012. "Developmental Risk of Depression: Experience Matters." *Child and Adolescent Psychiatric Clinics of North America* 21: 261–78.

Beck, A. T., A. J. Rush, B. F. Shaw, and G. Emory. 1979. *Cognitive Therapy of Depression.* New York: Guilford Press.

Beck, J. G. 1995. "Hypoactive Sexual Desire Disorder: An Overview." *Journal of Consulting and Clinical Psychology* 63 (6): 919–27.

Beck, J. G., and A. W. Bozman. 1995. "Gender Differences in Sexual Desire: The Effects of Anger and Anxiety." *Archives of Sexual Behavior* 24 (6): 595–612.

Bifulco, A., P. M. Moran, C. Ball, and O. Bernazzani. 2002. "Adult Attachment Style. I: Its Relationship to Clinical Depression." *Social Psychiatry and Psychiatric Epidemiology* 37 (2): 50–59.

Borkovec, T. D., and B. Sharpless. 2004. "Generalized Anxiety Disorder: Bringing Cognitive Behavioral Therapy into the Valued Present." In *Mindfulness and Acceptance: Expanding the Cognitive-Behavioral Tradition,* edited by S. C. Hayes, V. M. Follette, and M. M. Linehan. New York: Guilford Press.

Bowlby, J. 1988. *A Secure Base: Parent-Child Attachment and Healthy Human Development.* New York: Basic Books.

Bradbury, T. N., and F. D. Fincham. 1990. "Attributions in Marriage: Review and Critique." *Psychological Bulletin* 107 (1): 3–33.

Brown, G. W., and T. O. Harris. 1989. *Life Events and Illness.* New York: Guilford Press.

Byers, S. E. 2005. "Relationship Satisfaction and Sexual Satisfaction: A Longitudinal Study of Individuals in Long-Term Relationships." *The Journal of Sex Research* 42 (2): 113–18.

Campbell, L., J. A. Simpson, J. Boldry, and D. A. Kashy. 2005. "Perceptions of Conflict and Support in Romantic Relationships: The Role of Attachment Anxiety." *Journal of Personality and Social Psychology* 88 (3): 510–31.

Collins, N. L. 1996. "Working Models of Attachment: Implications for Explanation, Emotion, and Behavior." *Journal of Personality and Social Psychology* 71 (4): 810–32.

Cutrona, C. E., P. A. Shaffer, K. A. Wesner, and K. A. Gardner. 2007. "Optimally Matching Support and Perceived Spousal Sensitivity." *Journal of Family Psychology* 21 (4): 754–58.

Davidson, J. R., and S. E. Meltzer-Brody. 1999. "The Underrecognition and Undertreatment of Depression: What Is the Breadth and Depth of the Problem?" *Journal of Clinical Psychiatry* 60 (Suppl 7): 4–9.

Davila, J., and D. A. Kashy. 2009. "Secure Base Processes in Couples: Daily Associations Between Support Experiences and Attachment Security." *Journal of Family Psychology* 23 (1): 76–88.

Davila, J., T. N. Bradbury, C. L. Cohan, and S. Tochluk. 1997. "Marital Functioning and Depressive Symptoms: Evidence for a Stress Generation Model." *Journal of Personality and Social Psychology* 73 (4): 849–61.

DeWall, C. N., N. M. Lambert, E. B. Slotter, R. S. Pond Jr., T. Deckman, E. J. Finkel, L. B. Luchies, and F. D. Fincham. 2011. "So Far Away from One's Partner, Yet So Close to Romantic Alternatives: Avoidant Attachment, Interest in Alternatives, and Infidelity." *Journal of Personality and Social Psychology* 101 (6): 1302–16.

Dym, B. 1996. "Couple Therapy and Depression: Putting Odegaard's Method in Perspective." *Families, Systems, and Health* 14 (2): 183–87.

Eastwick, P. W., and E. J. Finkel. 2008. "The Attachment System in Fledgling Relationships: An Activating Role for Attachment Anxiety." *Journal of Personality and Social Psychology* 95 (3): 628–47.

Eaton, N. R., K. M. Keyes, R. F. Krueger, S. Balsis, A. E. Skodol, K. E. Markon, B. F. Grant, and D. S. Hasin. 2012. "An Invariant Dimensional Liability Model of Gender Differences in Mental Disorder Prevalence: Evidence from a National Sample." *Journal of Abnormal Psychology* 121 (1): 282–88.

Ein-Dor, T., and G. Hirschberger. 2012. "Sexual Healing: Daily Diary Evidence That Sex Relieves Stress for Men and Women in Satisfying Relationships." *Journal of Social and Personal Relationships* 29 (1): 126–39.

Elder, W. B., G. R. Brooks, and S. L. Morrow. 2012. "Sexual Self-Schemas of Heterosexual Men." *Psychology of Men and Masculinity* 13 (2): 166–79.

Emmons, R. A., and M. E. McCullough. 2003. "Counting Blessings Versus Burdens: An Experimental Investigation of Gratitude and Subjective Well-Being in Daily Life." *Journal of Personality and Social Psychology* 84 (2): 377–89.

Feeney, J. A., and P. Noller. 1990. "Attachment Style as a Predictor of Adult Romantic Relationships." *Journal of Personality and Social Psychology.* 58 (2): 281–91.

Fraley, R. C., and P. R. Shaver. 2000. "Adult Romantic Attachment: Theoretical Developments, Emerging Controversies, and Unanswered Questions." *Review of General Psychology* 4 (2): 132–54.

Fruzzetti, A. E., and K. M. Iverson. 2004. "Mindfulness, Acceptance, Validation, and 'Individual' Psychopathology in Couples." In *Mindfulness and Acceptance: Expanding the Cognitive-Behavioral Tradition*, edited by S. C. Hayes, V. M. Follette, and M. M. Linehan. New York: Guilford Press.

Gadassi, R., N. Mor, and E. Rafaeli. 2011. "Depression and Empathic Accuracy in Couples: An Interpersonal Model of Gender Differences in Depression." *Psychological Science* 22 (8): 1033–41.

Gilbert, P. 2009. *The Compassionate Mind: A New Approach to Facing the Challenges of Life.* London: Constable Robinson.

Goldfarb, M. R., G. Trudel, R. Boyer, and M. Préville. 2007. "Marital Relationship and Psychological Distress: Its Correlates and Treatments." *Sexual and Relationship Therapy* 22 (1): 109–26.

Gordon, A. M., E. A. Impett, A. Kogan, C. Oveis, and D. Keltner. 2012. "To Have and to Hold: Gratitude Promotes Relationship Maintenance in Intimate Bonds." *Journal of Personality and Social Psychology* 103 (2): 257–74.

Gottman, J. M., and N. Silver. 1999. *The Seven Principles for Making Marriage Work: A Practical Guide from the Country's Foremost Relationship Expert.* New York: Three Rivers Press.

Hayes, S. C., K. D. Strosahl, and K. G. Wilson. 1999. *Acceptance and Commitment Therapy: An Experiential Approach to Behavior Change*. New York: Guilford Press.

Hayes, S. C., K. D. Strosahl, K. G. Wilson, R. T. Bissett, J. Pistorello, D. Toarmino, et al. 2004. "Measuring Experiential Avoidance: A Preliminary Test of a Working Model." *The Psychological Record*. 54: 553–78.

Hazan, C., and P. Shaver. 1987. "Romantic Love Conceptualized as an Attachment Process." *Journal of Personality and Social Psychology* 52 (3): 511–24.

Heavey, C. L., C. Layne, and A. Christensen. 1993. "Gender and Conflict Structure in Marital Interaction: A Replication and Extension." *Journal of Consulting and Clinical Psychology* 61 (1): 16–27.

Hiller, J. 2006. "Loss of Sexual Interest and Negative States of Mind." In *Sex, Mind, and Emotion: Innovation in Psychological Theory and Practice*, edited by J. Hiller, H. Wood, and W. Bolton. London: Karnac Books.

Holahan, C. J., R. H. Moos, C. K. Holahan, P. L. Brennan, and K. K. Schutte. 2005. "Stress Generation, Avoidance Coping, and Depressive Symptoms: A Ten-Year Model." *Journal of Consulting and Clinical Psychology* 73 (4): 658–66.

Jacobson, N. S., A. E. Fruzzetti, K. Dobson, M. Whisman, and H. Hops. 1993. "Couple Therapy as a Treatment for Depression: II. The Effects of Relationship Quality and Therapy on Depressive Relapse." *Journal of Consulting and Clinical Psychology* 61 (3): 516–19.

Jinyao, Y., Z. Xiongzhao, R. P. Auerbach, C. K. Gardiner, C. Lin, W. Yuping, and Y. Shuqiao. 2012. "Insecure Attachment as a Predictor of Depressive and Anxious Symptomology." *Depression and Anxiety* 29 (9): 789–96.

Johnson, S. M. 2004. "Attachment Theory: A Guide for Healing Couple Relationships." In *Adult Attachment: Theory, Research, and Clinical Implications*, edited by W. S. Rholes and J. A. Simpson. New York: Guilford Press.

Kessler, R. C. 1997. "The Effects of Stressful Life Events on Depression." *Annual Review of Psychology* 48: 191–214.

Kessler, R. C., P. Berglund, O. Demler, R. Jin, and E. E. Walters. 2005. "Lifetime Prevalence and Age-of-Onset Distributions of *DSM–IV* Disorders in the National Comorbidity Survey Replication." *Archives of General Psychiatry* 62 (6): 593–602.

Kircanski, K., M. D. Lieberman, and M. G. Craske. 2012. "Feelings into Words: Contributions of Language to Exposure Therapy." *Psychological Science* 23 (10): 1086–91.

Klein, D. N., and N. J. Santiago. 2003. "Dysthymia and Chronic Depression: Introduction, Classification, Risk Factors, and Course." *Journal of Clinical Psychology* 59 (8): 807–16.

Klerman, G. L., M. M. Weissman, B. J. Rounsaville, and E. S. Chevron. 1984. *Interpersonal Psychotherapy of Depression.* New York: Basic Books.

Kunce, L. J., and P. R. Shaver. 1994. "An Attachment-Theoretical Approach to Caregiving in Romantic Relationships." In *Attachment Processes in Adulthood. Advances in Personal Relationships,* edited by K. Bartholomew and D. Perlman. London: Jessica Kingsley.

Leary, M. R., E. B. Tate, C. E. Adams, A. B. Allen, and J. Hancock. 2007. "Self-Compassion and Reactions to Unpleasant Self-Relevant Events: The Implications of Treating Oneself Kindly." *Journal of Personality and Social Psychology* 92 (5): 887–904.

Lieberman, M. D., T. K. Inagaki, G. Tabibnia, and M. J. Crockett. 2011. "Subjective Responses to Emotional Stimuli During Labeling, Reappraisal, and Distraction." *Emotion* 11 (3): 468–80.

Lincoln, T. M., F. Hohenhaus, and M. Hartmann. 2013. "Can Paranoid Thoughts Be Reduced by Targeting Negative Emotions and Self-Esteem? An Experimental Investigation of a Brief Compassion-Focused Intervention." *Cognitive Therapy and Research* 37 (2): 390–402.

Linehan, M. M. 1993. *Skills Training Manual for Treatment of Borderline Personality Disorder.* New York: Guilford Press.

Lopez, F. G. and B. Gormley. 2002. "Stability and Change in Adult Attachment Style over the First-Year College Transition: Relations to Self-Confidence, Coping, and Distress Patterns." *Journal of Counseling Psychology* 49 (3): 355–64.

Markowitz, J. C., and M. M. Weissman. 2004. "Interpersonal Psychotherapy: Principles and Applications." *World Psychiatry* 3 (3): 136–39.

Martel, C., M. Addis, and S. Dimidjian. 2004. "Finding the Action in Behavioral Action: The Search for Empirically Supported Interventions and Mechanisms of Change." In *Mindfulness and Acceptance: Expanding the Cognitive-Behavioral Tradition,* edited by S. C. Hayes, V. M. Follette, and M. M. Linehan. New York: Guilford Press.

McCarthy, B., and E. McCarthy. 2003. *Rekindling Desire.* New York: Brunner-Routledge.

McKay, M., P. Fanning, and P. Z. Ona. 2011. *Mind and Emotions: A Universal Treatment for Emotional Disorders.* Oakland: New Harbinger Publications.

McLeod, J. D. 1994. "Anxiety Disorders and Marital Quality." *Journal of Abnormal Psychology* 103 (4): 767–76.

Mikulincer, M., and P. R. Shaver. 2007. *Attachment in Adulthood: Structure, Dynamics, and Change.* New York: Guilford Press.

Monroe, S. M. 2010. "Recurrence in Major Depression: Assessing Risk Indicators in the Context of Risk Estimates." In *Relapse Prevention for Depression,* edited by C. S. Richards and M. G. Perri. Washington, DC: American Psychological Association.

Murray, S. L., D. W. Griffin, P. Rose, and G. M. Bellavia. 2003. "Calibrating the Sociometer: The Relational Contingencies of Self-Esteem." *Journal of Personality and Social Psychology* 85 (1): 63–84.

Neff, K. D. 2003. "Self-Compassion: An Alternative Conceptualization of a Healthy Attitude Toward Oneself." *Self and Identity* 2 (2): 85–101.

Neff, K. D., S. S. Rude, and K. L. Kirkpatrick. 2007. "An Examination of Self-Compassion in Relation to Positive Psychological Functioning and Personality Traits." *Journal of Research in Personality* 41 (4): 908–16.

Nolen-Hoeksema, S., and B. Jackson. 2001. "Mediators of the Gender Difference in Rumination." *Psychology of Women Quarterly* 25: 37–47.

Odegaard, P. 1996. "Empathy Induction in the Couple Treatment of Depression: Shifting the Focus from Self to Other." *Families, Systems, and Health* 14 (2): 167–81.

Partonen, T., and S. R. Pandi-Perumal. 2009. *Seasonal Affective Disorder: Practice and Research.* Oxford: Oxford University Press.

Perry, B. D. 2002. "Childhood Experience and the Expression of Genetic Potential: What Childhood Neglect Tells Us About Nature and Nurture." *Brain and Mind* 3 (1): 79–100.

Phillips, Jr., R. L., and J. R. Slaughter. 2000. "Depression and Sexual Desire." *American Family Physician* 62 (4): 782–86.

Proulx, C.M., C. Buehler, and H. Helms. 2009. "Moderators of the Link Between Marital Hostility and Change in Spouses' Depressive Symptoms." *Journal of Family Psychology* 23 (4): 540–50.

Rapaport, M. H. 2001. "Prevalence, Recognition, and Treatment of Comorbid Depression and Anxiety." *Journal of Clinical Psychiatry* 62 (Suppl 24): 6–10.

Rehman, U. S., A. H. Rellini, and E. Fallis. 2011. "The Importance of Sexual Self-Disclosure to Sexual Satisfaction and Functioning in Committed Relationships." *Journal of Sexual Medicine* 8 (11): 3108–15.

Reiss, S., and R. J. McNally. 1985. "Expectancy Model of Fear." In *Theoretical Issues in Behavior Therapy,* edited by S. Reiss and R. R. Bootzin. San Diego: Academic Press.

Rivas-Vazquez, R. A., D. Saffa-Biller, I. Ruiz, M. A. Blais, and A. Rivas-Vazquez. 2004. "Current Issues in Anxiety and Depression: Comorbid, Mixed, and Subthreshold Disorders." *Professional Psychology: Research and Practice* 35 (1): 74–83.

Saavedra, M. C., K. E. Chapman, and R. D. Rogge. 2010. "Clarifying Links Between Attachment and Relationship Quality: Hostile Conflict and Mindfulness as Moderators." *Journal of Family Psychology* 24 (4): 380–90.

Sanford, K. 2010. "Perceived Threat and Perceived Neglect: Couples' Underlying Concerns During Conflict." *Psychological Assessment* 22 (2): 288–97.

Sauer-Zavala, S., J. F. Boswell, M. W. Gallagher, K. H. Bentley, A. Ametaj, and D. H. Barlow. 2012. "The Role of Negative Affectivity and Negative Reactivity to Emotions in Predicting Outcomes in the Unified Protocol for the Transdiagnostic Treatment of Emotional Disorders." *Behaviour Research and Therapy* 50 (9): 551–57.

Schröder-Abé, M., and A. Schütz. 2011. "Walking in Each Other's Shoes: Perspective Taking Mediates Effects of Emotional Intelligence on Relationship Quality." *European Journal of Personality* 25 (2): 155–69.

Scott, R. L. and J. V. Cordova. 2002. "The Influence of Adult Attachment Styles on the Association Between Marital Adjustment and Depressive Symptoms." *Journal of Family Psychology* 16 (2): 199–208.

Segal, Z. V., J. D. Teasdale, and J. M. G. Williams. 2004. "Mindfulness-Based Cognitive Therapy: Theoretical Rationale and Empirical Status." In *Mindfulness and Acceptance: Expanding the Cognitive-Behavioral Tradition*, edited by S. C. Hayes, V. M. Follette, and M. M. Linehan. New York: Guilford Press.

Skowron, E. A. 2000. "The Role of Differentiation of Self in Marital Adjustment." *Journal of Counseling Psychology* 47 (2): 229–37.

Smith, D. A., M. J. Breiding, and L. M. Papp. 2012. "Depressive Moods and Marital Happiness: Within-Person Synchrony, Moderators, and Meaning." *Journal of Family Psychology* 26 (3): 338–47.

Sowislo, J. F., and U. Orth. 2013. "Does Low Self-Esteem Predict Depression and Anxiety? A Meta-Analysis of Longitudinal Studies." *Psychological Bulletin* 139 (1): 213–40.

Story, L. B., and R. Repetti. 2006. "Daily Occupational Stressors and Marital Behavior." *Journal of Family Psychology* 20 (4): 690–700.

Swami, V. 2012. "Mental Health Literacy of Depression: Gender Differences and Attitudinal Antecedents in a Representative British Sample." *PLoS ONE* 7 (11): e49779. doi:10.1371/journal.pone.0049779

Teyber, E., and F. McClure. 2011. *Interpersonal Process in Therapy: An Integrative Model*. Belmont, CA: Brooks/Cole.

Verplanken, B., and N. Fisher. 2013. "Habitual Worrying and Benefits of Mindfulness." *Mindfulness* (April 11). doi: 10.1007/s12671-013-0211-0.

Watson, L. 2012. *Wanting Sex Again: How to Rediscover Your Desire and Heal a Sexless Marriage.* New York: Penguin Group.

Weissman, M. M., J. C. Markowitz, and G. L. Klerman. 2000. *Comprehensive Guide to Interpersonal Psychotherapy.* New York: Basic Books.

Whisman, M. A. 2001. "The Association Between Depression and Marital Dissatisfaction." In *Marital and Family Processes in Depression: A Scientific Foundation for Clinical Practice,* edited by S. R. H. Beach. Washington, DC: American Psychological Association.

Yeh, H., F. O. Lorenz, K. A. S. Wickrama, R. D. Conger, and G. H. Elder Jr. 2006. "Relationships Among Sexual Satisfaction, Marital Quality, and Marital Instability at Midlife." *Journal of Family Psychology* 20 (2): 339–43.

Young, M., G. Denny, R. Luquis, and T. Young. 1998. "Correlates of Sexual Satisfaction in Marriage." *Canadian Journal of Human Sexuality* 7 (2): 115–27.

Photograph by Stephanie Cristalli

Shannon Kolakowski, PsyD, is a licensed psychologist in private practice. She blogs for *Huffington Post* and has been featured in magazines such as *Redbook, ParentMap,* and *Men's Health Magazine,* as well as online at Shape.com and eHarmony. She's made television appearances on *New Day Northwest* and *ABC News.* Her expertise lies in combining the latest research with her personal insight, experience, and passion for the practice of psychology. She lives with her husband in Seattle, WA. Visit her online at www.drshannonk.com.

Foreword writer **Craig Malkin, PhD**, is a clinical psychologist, author, and instructor of psychology at Harvard Medical School. His articles and insights have frequently been featured in publications like *Psychology Today,* Match.com's *Happen Magazine,* and *Women's Health.* He's made numerous television and radio appearances, including appearances on National Public Radio and Fox News.

FROM OUR PUBLISHER—

As the publisher at New Harbinger and a clinical psychologist since 1978, I know that emotional problems are best helped with evidence-based therapies. These are the treatments derived from scientific research (randomized controlled trials) that show what works. Whether these treatments are delivered by trained clinicians or found in a self-help book, they are designed to provide you with proven strategies to overcome your problem.

Therapies that aren't evidence-based—whether offered by clinicians or in books—are much less likely to help. In fact, therapies that aren't guided by science may not help you at all. That's why this New Harbinger book is based on scientific evidence that the treatment can relieve emotional pain.

This is important: if this book isn't enough, and you need the help of a skilled therapist, use the following resources to find a clinician trained in the evidence-based protocols appropriate for your problem. And if you need more support—a community that understands what you're going through and can show you ways to cope—resources for that are provided below, as well.

Real help is available for the problems you have been struggling with. The skills you can learn from evidence-based therapies will change your life.

Matthew McKay, PhD
Publisher, New Harbinger Publications

new harbinger
CELEBRATING
40 YEARS

**If you need a therapist, the following organization
can help you find a therapist trained in cognitive behavioral therapy (CBT).**

The Association for Behavioral & Cognitive Therapies (ABCT) Find-a-Therapist service offers a list of therapists schooled in CBT techniques. Therapists listed are licensed professionals who have met the membership requirements of ABCT and who have chosen to appear in the directory.

Please visit www.abct.org and click on *Find a Therapist*.

For additional support for patients, family, and friends, please contact the following:

Anxiety and Depression Association of America (ADAA) **Visit www.adaa.org**

National Alliance on Mental Illness (NAMI) **Visit www.nami.org**

Depression and Bipolar Support Alliance (DBSA) **Visit www.dbsalliance.org**

National Suicide Prevention Lifeline
Call 24 hours a day 1-800-273-TALK (8255) or visit suicidepreventionlifeline.org

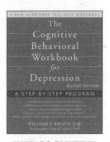
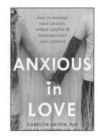
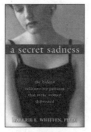

Register your **new harbinger** titles for additional benefits!

When you register your **new harbinger** title—purchased in any format, from any source—you get access to benefits like the following:

- Downloadable accessories like printable worksheets and extra content

- Instructional videos and audio files

- Information about updates, corrections, and new editions

Not every title has accessories, but we're adding new material all the time.

Access free accessories in 3 easy steps:

1. Sign in at NewHarbinger.com (or **register** to create an account).

2. Click on **register a book**. Search for your title and click the **register** button when it appears.

3. Click on the **book cover or title** to go to its details page. Click on **accessories** to view and access files.

That's all there is to it!

If you need help, visit:

NewHarbinger.com/accessories

new harbinger
CELEBRATING
40 YEARS